Letts

Revise GCSE

French

includes audio CD

Terry Murray

Contents

4 Holidays

5 Home, local area and environment

6 Education and work

This book and

Stay on course! Use these pages to get to know your course.

No matter which exam board you are using, you have to do...
- a listening and a reading exam
- two controlled writing assessments
- two controlled speaking assessments.

For your listening and reading exams, your teacher will enter you for either Foundation or Higher:
- If you do Higher, your grade for that skill will be from A* to E.
- If you do Foundation, your grade for that skill will be from C to G.

In your speaking and writing controlled assessments, you are not entered for Foundation or Higher. Your final mark in these controlled assessments depends on how well you do. This is called 'differentiation by outcome'.

Here are some guidelines on the length of the exams and controlled assessments:

Listening Foundation
An exam lasting 30–40 minutes.
Listening Higher
An exam lasting 40–50 minutes.
Reading Foundation
An exam lasting 30–40 minutes.
Reading Higher
An exam lasting 40–50 minutes.
Speaking
Two controlled assessments lasting four to six minutes each.
Writing
Two controlled assessments lasting about an hour each.

Individual exam boards' topic areas are shown opposite.

AQA

Lifestyle
Health:
- Healthy and unhealthy lifestyles and their consequences

Relationships and choices:
- Relationships with family and friends
- Future plans regarding marriage/partnership
- Social issues and equality

Leisure
Free time and the media:
- Free time activities
- Shopping, money, fashion and trends
- Advantages and disadvantages of new technology

Holidays:
- Plans, preferences, experiences
- What to see and getting around

Home and environment
Home and local area:
- Special occasions celebrated in the home
- Home, town, neighbourhood and region: where it is and what it is like

Environment:
- Current problems facing the planet
- Being environmentally friendly within the home and local area

Work and education
School/college and future plans:
- What school/college is like
- Pressures and problems

Current and future jobs:
- Looking for and getting a job
- Advantages and disadvantages of different jobs

OCR

Topic area 1 – Home and local area
- Life in the home, friends and relationships
- Local area, facilities and getting around

Topic area 2 – Health and sport
- Sport, outdoor pursuits and healthy lifestyle
- Food and drink as aspects of culture and health

Topic area 3 – Leisure and entertainment (includes online)
- Socialising, special occasions and festivals
- TV, films and music

Topic area 4 – Travel and the wider world
- Holidays and exchanges
- Environmental, cultural and social issues

Topic area 5 – Education and work
- School life in the UK and in the target language country or community
- Work experience, future study and jobs, working abroad

Visit your awarding body's website for full course details or download your complete GCSE specifications.

your GCSE course

EDEXCEL

Speaking and writing
1. Media and culture
- Music/film/reading
- Fashion/celebrities/religion
- Blogs/Internet

2. Sport and leisure
- Hobbies/interests
- Sporting events
- Lifestyle choices

3. Travel and tourism
- Holidays
- Accommodation
- Eating, food, drink

4. Business, work and employment
- Work experience/part-time jobs
- Product or service information

5. Centre-devised option

Listening and reading
Out and about
- Visitor information
- Basic weather
- Local amenities
- Accommodation
- Public transport
- Directions

Customer service and transactions
- Cafés and restaurants
- Shops
- Dealing with problems

Personal information
- General interests
- Leisure activities
- Family and friends
- Lifestyle (healthy eating and exercise)

Future plans, education and work
- Basic language of the Internet
- Simple job advertisements
- Simple job applications and CVs
- School and college
- Work and work experience

WJEC

Personal and social life
- Self, family, friends, home life, shopping, meals, healthy living, illness and accidents, free time, fashion, relationships, future plans.

Local community
- Home town, school, education, local environment, pollution, recycling, local facilities, comparisons with other towns and regions, weather and seasons.

The world of work
- Work experience, part-time jobs, future careers, technology (sending messages, accessing information).

The wider world
- Travel and holidays, media, social issues (e.g. life of young people today, homelessness, crime, drugs, healthy living, religion, politics), life in the countries and communities where the language is spoken.

CCEA

Context 1: The individual – Students' lives, families, homes and interests, and those of others in French-speaking countries and communities
- Relationships: families and friends
- Local environment: advantages and disadvantages
- Activities: daily routine and leisure activities
- Health and lifestyle: diet, exercise and illness

Context 2: Citizenship – Lifestyles, attitudes and customs in students' own countries and communities, and in French-speaking countries and communities
- Social issues: problems in society and equality
- Travel and tourism: destinations and choices
- Environmental issues: attitudes to and responsibilities for litter, transport, energy, conservation and recycling
- Media and communications
- Celebrations: festivals and customs

Context 3: Employability – Education and employment in students' own countries and communities, and in French-speaking countries and communities
- School life
- Part-time jobs: advantages and disadvantages
- Future plans: choices and expectations

www.aqa.org.uk, www.ocr.org.uk, www.edexcel.com, www.wjec.co.uk, www.ccea.org.uk

A student's guide to the speaking and writing controlled assessments

How many controlled assessments do I have to do?
Two for speaking and two for writing.

When will I be doing my controlled assessments?
Anytime in Year 9, 10 or 11. Your teacher can choose the time.

How long are the controlled assessments?
Each speaking assessment will last four to six minutes (WJEC: four to seven minutes). The writing assessment will be a minimum of 200 words, spread over the two pieces, but you should aim for 400–600 words, spread over the two pieces, if you want at least a grade C. Each writing assessment must be done in an hour.

When do I start preparing?
There are three stages:

Stage 1: Your teacher will prepare you for the task. He/she cannot tell you at this stage what the task is, but you should be able to guess it!

Stage 2: The teacher gives you the task. After this, the teacher cannot give you any language guidance, but he/she can tell you that past tenses are to be used here and future tenses there, for example. Stage 2 can last for anything from a few days to most of a term, depending on the exam board:

AQA	Six hours including lesson time and homework time
OCR	Two hours of class time
EDEXCEL	Speaking: two weeks and no more than six hours of contact time Writing: No limit
WJEC	Two weeks
CCEA	Speaking: three to four hours. Writing: five to six hours

Stage 3: This is when you do the controlled assessment.

Can I ask my teacher to extend the deadline?
No.

What if I do an awful piece of controlled assessment?
Your teacher will let you do another one but it must be a different task.

Can I use ICT?
In the controlled writing assessment, you can write your work on a computer but it will take place in exam conditions.

> It is very clear that many GCSE candidates write less well using ICT. In particular, they tend to be less accurate and leave out more accents when they type. So use word-processing with care.

Can I use electronic translators?
No. In the controlled speaking assessment, you will have access to your cue card of 30–40 words. In the controlled writing assessment, you will have access to your cue card of 30–40 words and a dictionary. This can be an online dictionary.

Do I get marks for presentation?
No – if you write a brochure, for example, you will not get any marks for pictures and maps (even if you draw them yourself). Similarly, do not waste time on title pages, fancy borders, folders and so on.

> You should always take care to make all your work neat and easy to read.

Can I do the same piece of speaking or writing as other people in my class?
Yes, and you will probably use quite a lot of the same vocabulary and structures as well. But there will always be differences as you will be speaking or writing about your holiday or your work experience, for example.

Can I use a writing frame?

In Stage 1 and 2, yes. However, the more of your own ideas you write, the higher your marks are likely to be.

Can I use pieces of writing I have seen in books?

You must never, ever copy. However, you should try to use lots of interesting vocabulary and phrases you have learned from your worksheets and coursebooks.

Can I get other people to help me?

No – you and your teacher have to sign that this is your own, unaided controlled assessment. You will cover all of the language you need in class and you will be helped with your planning. Your teacher will have a good idea of the standard of writing you are capable of from your other work in class. If your teacher suspects you have not written a piece of controlled assessment yourself, he/she might...

- refuse to let you submit it at all
- make you rewrite the piece in exam conditions
- inform the exam board that you have been cheating.

> It is very easy for teachers and examiners to spot where a candidate has tried to write their own French and where they have copied, so don't do it. The Internet websites that advertise materials usually offer mistake-littered work.

Planning your study

Make sure that you have learned all the necessary words after you complete each topic. You could draw a mind map or create a database on your PC. During the topic try to learn 10 new words a day. Ask someone to test you on the words: you need to be able to spell the words properly, and use accents correctly, so remember to write them down when being tested.

- Each chapter in the book includes sample conversations. These conversations will help you to prepare for your controlled assessments in speaking. You might like to read the conversations with a friend and/or make a recording of the conversations. You could then listen to the conversations as part of your revision plan. This will boost your fluency.
- Practise the questions in the book. This will build your confidence and enable you to anticipate the type of questions that will occur in the GCSE examination.
- Decide if you know the topic thoroughly and if there are any weak areas: note them and look for ways to improve on them in the next topic, e.g. use of adjectives, use of the past tense.

How this book will help you

This Letts *Revise GCSE French Study and Revision Guide* will help you because...

- it contains the essential vocabulary and grammatical structures needed for the GCSE course.
- it contains progress checks as well as GCSE questions to help you to check and reaffirm your understanding.
- there are examples of controlled assessment tasks with model answers and advice from an examiner on how to get them right. Translations are provided on pages 155–156 to aid understanding.
- trying the exam practice questions will give you the opportunity to make use of the vocabulary that you have learned and will give you a measure of your progress.
- examiner's hints and key points are used throughout the chapters to help you. Use these as your signposts to guide you to success in your GCSE course.

32 points for improving your grade

Do not try to include all 32 points – 15 to 20 will be fine.

Listed below are 32 points that will help to improve the quality of language in your speaking and writing work and raise your grade in the controlled assessments. Try to include a good number of these points in your work.

Examples of these points being used are shown where you see this icon , on the 'Sample controlled assessment' pages throughout this book.

1   Use an **avoir** structure, e.g.:

avoir besoin de	to need
J'avais besoin d'un bon prof.	I needed a good teacher.
avoir envie de	to want, to feel like
J'ai envie d'aller en France.	I want to go to France.
en avoir marre	to be fed up
J'en avais marre.	I was fed up with it.
avoir lieu	to take place
Un accident a eu lieu.	There was an accident/An accident took place.

2   Try to include at least three uses of **parce que**, e.g.:
Je suis allé(e) en France parce que j'aime la cuisine.
I went to France because I like the food.

3   Try to include at least two justified points of view, e.g.:
Je crois que la France est le meilleur pays du monde parce que la cuisine y est tellement bonne.
I think that France is the best country in the world because the food is so good there.

4   Use **j'ai décidé de...** (I decided to...)

5   Use **sans** + the infinitive, e.g.:

sans hésiter	without hesitating
sans perdre de temps	without wasting any time

6   Use **avant de...**, e.g.:

avant d'arriver	before arriving
avant de manger	before eating

7   Use **en** + the present participle, e.g.:

en arrivant	on arriving
en le voyant	on seeing him

8   Use **après avoir** + the past participle, e.g.:

Après avoir mangé, je...	After eating, I...

9   Use exclamations, e.g.:

Quelle bonne idée!	What a good idea!
Quel désastre!	What a disaster!

10   Try to include at least three uses of the present tense.

11   Try to include at least four perfect tenses: one using **avoir**, one using **être**, one reflexive and one with an irregular past participle.

12 Try to include at least three future tenses, including an irregular.

13 Use an imperfect, e.g.:

Il pleuvait.   It was raining.

14 Use a conditional, e.g.:

je serais   I would be

15 Don't forget to include adjectives, e.g.:

Une expérience inoubliable	An unforgettable experience
Un temps affreux	Terrible weather
Un professeur superbe	A superb teacher

16 Try to use impressive vocabulary and structures, e.g.:

Je passe deux heures à faire mes devoirs.

I spend two hours doing my homework.

de très bon matin

very early in the morning

Je ramasse même des papiers.

I even pick up litter.

17 Use a pluperfect, e.g.:

J'avais déjà fait sa connaissance.	I had already met him.
qu'on m'avait promis	that I had been promised

18 Use **vraiment**, **si** or **tellement** (so/really) instead of **très**, e.g.:

vraiment important	really important
vraiment utile	really useful

19 Use **malgré** (in spite of), e.g.:

malgré le fait que   in spite of the fact that

20 Use **venir de** (to have just), e.g.:

Je viens de commencer à apprendre une nouvelle langue.

I have just started learning a new language.

21 Use **sur le point de** (on the point of/about to), e.g.:

J'étais sur le point de faire mes devoirs...

I was just about to do my homework...

22 Use comparatives, e.g.:

plus beau que	more handsome than
moins fort que	not as strong as
aussi intelligent que	as intelligent as
moins joli que	not as pretty as

23 Use superlatives, e.g.:

le plus beau	the finest
le moins agréable	the least pleasant

24 Use negatives, e.g.:

Je ne le fais plus.   I do not do it anymore.

25 Try to use a subjunctive (this is an A-level structure but you can get extra marks by using examples), e.g.:

Il faut que je fasse la vaisselle.	I have to do the washing-up.
Il faut que j'aille chez ma grand-mère.	I have to go to my grandmother's.

26 Use **depuis** (since), e.g.:

J'habite ici depuis quinze ans.   I have lived here for 15 years.

27 Try to reduce the number of simple verbs such as **je m'appelle**, **je suis** and **j'ai**.

28 Try to use full descriptions (i.e. 10 pieces of information).

29 Try not to repeat any verb.

30 Use connecting words (connectives), e.g.:

qui, que	who, which, that
tandis que	whilst, whereas
car	for, because
lorsque	when
puisque	since, because

31 Use **pour** + the infinitive, e.g.:

Pour voir mon ami...   In order to see my friend...

32 Use pronouns, e.g.:

Il m'a accompagné.   He came with me.

In the piece of work below, the student has implemented most of the 32 points. This piece of work would be worth an A*. The numbers in the text refer to the points outlined above.

School

The '32 points for improving your grade' are referenced in the passages on the 'Sample controlled assessment' pages in the same way as they appear in this example.

Malheureusement[16] il faut que j'aille[25] au lit à neuf heures du soir pour pouvoir[31] me lever à six heures. En me levant,[7] je prends une douche, et après avoir pris[8] mon petit déjeuner, je sors le plus vite possible[23] pour prendre le car. Je viens de[20] faire la connaissance de Pierre et normalement il m'accompagne.[32] Je le connais depuis deux semaines.[26] En arrivant[7] au collège, je retrouve mes amis et j'ai cinq cours. Malheureusement, je ne supporte plus[24] l'histoire.

Hier au collège, quel désastre![9] J'étais sur le point de commencer[21] mon premier cours - la pire matière[23] - histoire! - quand j'ai découvert que j'avais laissé[17] tous mes livres à la maison. Sans perdre de temps,[5] j'ai téléphoné à mon frère aîné[16] et il me les[32] a apportés en voiture.

Mais le prof m'a grondé.[16] J'en ai marre![1] Le prof est si sévère.[18] J'ai décidé de[4] laisser tomber l'histoire puisque le prof me gronde tout le temps.

Demain, j'aurai[12] ma meilleure matière - l'espagnol. Je crois que c'est la matière la plus importante parce que l'espagnol est tellement utile[18] partout dans le monde entier. Un jour, je serai[12] prof d'espagnol. Cela serait merveilleux...[14]

Tips for listening and reading

In the listening exam, first read the question carefully and highlight the question word so that you know the information that you are listening for. Use any visuals to help you to predict what you might hear. Try to anticipate the answer and note down possible words to listen for. Check numbers, dates and times very carefully.

In the reading exam, read the questions before you read the passage. Some words look like English words – you should try to work out their meaning.

It pays to think logically in both the reading and listening exams. Sometimes you have to use your common sense to work out the answers from the information given. Examiners will also test your knowledge of synonyms and related families of words, e.g. **Susanne aime bien lire** may become **Susanne adore la lecture**. Ensure that you know synonyms and families of nouns and verbs. Make a list of synonyms, near-synonyms and word families and learn them carefully, e.g. **le voyage** = **le trajet**.

1 Lifestyle and health

The following topics are covered in this chapter:

- Healthy and unhealthy lifestyles
- Food and drink
- Accidents and incidents
- Grammar

1.1 Healthy and unhealthy lifestyles

LEARNING SUMMARY

After studying this section, you should be able to:

- describe how to keep fit and healthy
- talk about your diet

Healthy lifestyles

AQA	✓
OCR	✓
EDEXCEL	✓
WJEC	✓
CCEA	✓

> Note how the sentences in 'Lifestyles' tend to start with different structures. Using a variety of structures gains extra marks in the controlled assessments.

The following sentences contain vocabulary and structures that will help you in the listening and reading exams, and in the controlled assessment.

Lifestyles

Voici des conseils pour rester en forme et éviter une crise cardiaque.
Here is some advice about staying fit and avoiding a heart attack.
Il faut éviter les maladies grâce à une vie mieux équilibrée.
We must avoid illness by leading a more balanced life.
Les maladies du coeur liées à une mauvaise alimentation font des milliers de morts.
Heart disease caused by bad diet causes thousands of deaths.
L'obésité touche un enfant sur six.
One child in six is obese.
Je vais manger sain.
I am going to eat a healthy diet.
Je varierai mes menus.
I will vary my diet.
La quantité de fruits et légumes que je consomme est importante.
The amount of fruit and vegetables I eat is important.
Je mangerai au moins cinq fruits et légumes par jour.
I will eat at least five portions of fruit and vegetables a day.
Je pratiquerai une activité régulière.
I will exercise regularly.

J'éviterai de manger trop gras ou trop sucré.

I will avoid a diet that is too fat or too sweet.

Je ne devrais pas fumer.

I should not smoke.

Je devrais me coucher de bonne heure.

I should go to bed early.

J'ai besoin de dormir huit heures minimum.

I need to sleep for a minimum of eight hours.

Je ne vais pas boire de l'alcool.

I am not going to drink alcohol.

Je voudrais changer mes habitudes.

I would like to change my habits.

Je désire aller au gymnase, faire de l'exercice et jouer au foot.

I want to go to the gym, do exercise and play football.

Je veux manger de la nourriture plus saine.

I want to eat healthier food.

Je préférerais manger plus de carottes, moins de graisse et de frites, et prendre des vitamines.

I would prefer to eat more carrots, less fat and fewer chips, and take vitamins.

On ne doit pas passer des heures à regarder la télé.

You must not spend too much time watching TV.

Il ne faut pas se nourrir de chips et de frites.

You must not just live off crisps and chips.

Il faut sortir et respirer l'air frais.

You must get out into the open air.

PROGRESS CHECK

Say or write the following in French:
1. A more balanced life
2. The open air
3. Healthier food
4. I should not smoke.
5. Avoid a heart attack.

1. Une vie mieux équilibrée
2. L'air frais
3. De la nourriture plus saine
4. Je ne devrais pas fumer.
5. Éviter une crise cardiaque.

1.2 Food and drink

LEARNING SUMMARY

After studying this section, you should be able to:

- talk about food and drink
- say what you like and do not like to eat and drink

Eating and drinking

AQA	✓
OCR	✓
EDEXCEL	✓
WJEC	✓
CCEA	✓

The topic of food and drink is regularly tested in the listening and reading exams. In the controlled speaking assessment, you might have to talk about what food and drink you like and dislike.

le pique-nique

Meals (Les repas)

le déjeuner – lunch
le dîner – dinner
le goûter – afternoon snack
la nourriture – food

le petit déjeuner – breakfast
le pique-nique – picnic
le repas – meal

Vegetables (Les légumes)

la carotte – carrot
le champignon – mushroom
le chou – cabbage
les frites (f, pl) – chips
le haricot vert – French bean
le légume – vegetable

l'oignon (m) – onion
le petit pois – pea
la pomme de terre – potato
le riz – rice
la salade – salad, lettuce
la tomate – tomato

Fruit (Les fruits)

la fraise

l'abricot (m) – apricot
l'ananas (m) – pineapple
la banane – banana
la cerise – cherry
le citron – lemon
la fraise – strawberry
la framboise – raspberry

le melon – melon
l'orange (f) – orange
la pêche – peach
la poire – pear
la pomme – apple
le raisin – grape
le raisin sec – raisin

Meat (La viande)

l'agneau (m) – lamb
le bifteck – steak
le bœuf – beef
le canard – duck
le jambon – ham
le porc – pork

le poulet – chicken
la saucisse – sausage
le saucisson – salami-type sausage
le steak – steak
le veau – veal

On the table (Sur la table)

le sel

l'assiette (f) – plate
le bol – bowl
la carafe d'eau – jug of water
la cafetière – coffee pot
le couteau – knife
la cuiller/la cuillère – spoon
la fourchette – fork
la moutarde – mustard

la nappe – tablecloth
le poivre – pepper
la sauce au jus de viande – gravy
le sel – salt
la soucoupe – saucer
le sucre – sugar
la tasse – cup
le verre – glass

Fish/seafood (Les poissons/les fruits de mer)

le crabe – crab

les crevettes (f, pl) – prawns

les huîtres (f, pl) – oysters

la morue – cod (salted, dried)

les moules (f, pl) – mussels

la sardine – sardine

le saumon – salmon

la truite – trout

le crabe

les huîtres

le saumon

Snacks (Les snacks)

le bonbon – sweet

les chips (f, pl) – crisps

le chocolat – chocolate

le croque-monsieur – toasted cheese sandwich with ham

l'omelette (f) – omelette

le sandwich – sandwich

le bonbon

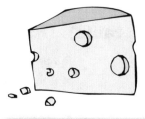

le sandwich

Desserts (Les desserts)

la crêpe – pancake

le dessert – dessert

le fromage – cheese

le gâteau – cake

la glace – ice cream

la pâtisserie – pastry

le yaourt – yoghurt

le fromage

la glace

le yaourt

Breakfast (Le petit déjeuner)

la baguette – French stick

le beurre – butter

les céréales (f, pl) – cereal

la confiture – jam

le croissant – croissant

le pain grillé – toast

le miel – honey

l'œuf à la coque (m) – boiled egg

le pain – bread

Drinks (Les boissons)

la **bière** – beer
la **boisson** – drink
le **café** – coffee
le **café-crème** – white coffee
le **chocolat chaud** – hot chocolate
le **cidre** – cider
le **citron pressé** – freshly-squeezed lemon
le **coca** – cola

l'**eau (f)** – water
l'**eau minérale (f)** – mineral water
le **jus de fruit** – fruit juice
le **lait** – milk
la **limonade** – lemonade
le **sirop** – cordial
le **thé** – tea
le **vin** – wine

Conversation: Grade C

AQA ✓
OCR ✓
EDEXCEL ✓
WJEC ✓
CCEA ✓

À quelle heure prends-tu le petit déjeuner?
Je mange le petit déjeuner à sept heures.
Qu'est-ce que tu manges?
Je mange du pain grillé et un œuf.
Quel est ton fruit préféré?
Je préfère les pommes.
Quel est ton légume préféré?
J'adore les frites!
Quelle est ta viande préférée?
J'aime bien l'agneau.
Qu'est-ce que tu aimes comme sandwich?
Je préfère les sandwichs au jambon.
Et comme snack, qu'est-ce que tu manges?
Je mange du chocolat.
Qu'est-ce que tu aimes comme dessert?
J'aime bien les glaces.
Quel parfum préfères-tu?
Je préfère les glaces à la fraise.
Qu'est-ce que tu aimes boire?
J'aime boire du coca.
Et avec ton petit déjeuner?
Je bois du thé.
Tu aimes le vin?
Je déteste le vin.
Qu'est-ce que tu as mangé aujourd'hui?
Ce matin, j'ai mangé des petits pains et ce soir je mangerai un steak.

le garçon

In the restaurant (Au restaurant)

l'**addition (f)** – bill
la **bouteille** – bottle
le **garçon** – waiter
le **menu (à 12 euros)** – (12-euro) menu
le **patron** – the boss
le **plat** – dish
le **plat du jour** – dish of the day, today's menu

le **pourboire** – tip
le **serveur/la serveuse** – waiter/waitress
le **service non compris** – service not included
les **toilettes (f, pl)** – toilets
le/la **végétarien(ne)** – vegetarian

Adjectives and phrases

Bon appétit! – Enjoy your meal!

bon marché – cheap

bruyant(e) – noisy

célèbre – famous

bien cuit(e) – well-done (steak)

délicieux (-ieuse) – delicious

frais (fraîche) – cool, fresh

à point – medium (steak)

le plat principal – main course

saignant(e) – rare (steak)

sensass – sensational

se disputer

Verbs

boire – to drink

changer – to change

commander – to order

se disputer – to argue

manger – to eat

préférer – to prefer

recommander – to recommend

servir – to serve

se tromper – to make a mistake

PROGRESS CHECK

Say or write the following in French:

1. Knife, fork and spoon
2. Seafood
3. I love chips.
4. I prefer strawberry ice cream.
5. Yoghurt

1. Le couteau, la fourchette et la cuillère
2. Les fruits de mer
3. J'adore les frites.
4. Je préfère les glaces à la fraise.
5. Le yaourt

1.3 Accidents and incidents

LEARNING SUMMARY

After studying this section, you should be able to:

● describe your own (or someone else's) state of health

● refer to particular health problems

● explain how accidents happened

● describe incidents such as theft

Health

AQA	✓
OCR	✓
EDEXCEL	✓
WJEC	✓
CCEA	✓

The topic health is frequently examined in the listening and reading exams. It may also figure in your controlled assessment for speaking and writing.

les yeux

les cheveux

l'oreille

le nez

la joue

la bouche

le cou

The body (Le corps)

la bouche – mouth	**la figure** – face	**l'oreille (f)** – ear
le bras – arm	**le genou** – knee	**l'os (m)** – bone
les cheveux (m, pl) – hair	**la gorge** – throat	**la peau** – skin
le cœur – heart	**la jambe** – leg	**le pied** – foot
le cou – neck	**la joue** – cheek	**le sang** – blood
le coude – elbow	**la langue** – tongue	**la tête** – head
la dent – tooth	**la lèvre** – lip	**le ventre** – stomach
le doigt – finger	**la main** – hand	**le visage** – face
le dos – back	**le menton** – chin	**la voix** – voice
l'épaule (f) – shoulder	**le nez** – nose	**les yeux (m, pl)** – eyes
l'estomac (m) – stomach	**l'œil (m)** – eye	

Health and illness (La santé et la maladie)

l'ambulance

l'ambulance (f) – ambulance	**malade** – sick
de l'aspirine (f) – aspirin	**la médecine/le médicament** – medicine
le comprimé – tablet	**l'ordonnance (f)** – prescription
le coup de soleil – sunstroke	**le pansement** – dressing
la douleur – pain	**la pilule** – pill
enrhumé – having a cold	**la piqûre** – sting
la fièvre – fever, temperature	**le rhume** – cold
la grippe – flu	**le sparadrap** – plaster

Verbs and phrases

avoir mal à l'estomac – to have stomach ache	**la blessure** – injury
avoir mal à l'oreille – to have earache	**se casser** – to break
avoir mal à la gorge – to have a sore throat	**se couper** – to cut oneself
avoir le mal de mer – to be seasick	**se faire mal** – to hurt oneself
avoir mal à la tête – to have a headache	**garder le lit** – to stay in bed
le blessé – injured person	**mourir** – to die
se blesser – to hurt oneself	**piquer** – to sting
	se sentir – to feel
	vomir – to vomit

Conversation

AQA	✓
OCR	✓
EDEXCEL	✓
WJEC	✓
CCEA	✓

🗣 **Les vacances, ça s'est bien passé?**
🗣 Non, j'étais malade.
🗣 **Qu'est-ce que tu avais?**
🗣 J'avais mal à l'estomac.
🗣 **Tu es allé(e) chez le médecin?**
🗣 Oui, il m'a donné une ordonnance.

Accidents and incidents

AQA	✓
OCR	✓
EDEXCEL	✓
WJEC	✓
CCEA	✓

un incendie

Accidents/incidents (Les accidents/les incidents)

l'assurance (f) – insurance

au feu! – fire!

le cambriolage – burglary

le cambrioleur – burglar

la collision – collision

crevé – punctured

le danger – danger

l'explosion (f) – explosion

l'incendie (m) – fire

tuer – to kill

voler – to steal

le voleur – thief

Verbs

aider – to help

aller chercher – to fetch

aller mieux – to be better

cambrioler – to burgle

faire de l'autostop – to hitchhike

freiner – to brake

glisser – to slip, to slide, to skid

se noyer – to drown

perdre – to lose

renverser – to knock over

Conversation

AQA	✓
OCR	✓
EDEXCEL	✓
WJEC	✓
CCEA	✓

Tu as vu l'accident?

Oui. Il y a eu une collision entre une voiture et un camion.

Il y a eu des blessés?

Le chauffeur du camion s'est cassé le bras et l'automobiliste s'est coupé au visage.

PROGRESS CHECK

Say or write the following in French:

1. I have a headache.
2. I have a cold.
3. I have toothache.
4. The car braked.
5. The lorry killed a child.
6. I must stay in bed.

6. Je dois garder le lit.
5. Le camion a tué un enfant.
4. La voiture a freiné.
3. J'ai mal aux dents.
2. Je suis enrhumé(e).
1. J'ai mal à la tête.

1.4 Grammar

LEARNING SUMMARY	After studying this section, you should be able to understand:
	• grammatical terms
	• the indefinite article
	• the definite article
	• the partitive article

Grammatical terms

AQA	✓
OCR	✓
EDEXCEL	✓
WJEC	✓
CCEA	✓

Before you start your grammar revision, you need to familiarise yourself with some grammatical terms. You will find this section useful to refer back to.

Look at this sentence:
The girl quickly makes a delicious cake in the kitchen.

The	definite article
girl	noun (subject)
quickly	adverb
makes	verb
a	indefinite article
delicious	adjective
cake	noun (direct object)
in	preposition
the	definite article
kitchen	noun

- The definite article is the grammatical name given to the word 'the'.
- The indefinite article is the name given to the word 'a' or 'an'.
- A noun is a person, place, thing or animal (e.g. Tom, London, chair, cat).
- A verb is a word that describes an action (e.g. eats, slept, is going).
- An adjective is a word that describes a noun (e.g. pretty, old, blue).
- An adverb is a word that describes a verb. It tells you how an action is done (e.g. quickly, nicely, easily). Many adverbs in English end in '-ly'.
- A preposition is a word placed before a noun or a pronoun to indicate time, place or condition (e.g. on the table).
- A conjunction is a word that links two parts of a sentence (e.g. 'He was eating and drinking'). The most common conjunctions in English are 'and' and 'but'.
- A pronoun is a word that stands in place of a noun. In the sentence above, we could replace the noun 'the girl' by the pronoun 'she'. Similarly, 'a cake' could be replaced by 'it'.
- A relative pronoun is a word that links one part of a sentence to another. In English, the relative pronouns are 'who', 'whom', 'which', 'where' and 'that' (e.g. 'I gave him all the money that I earned'). The two parts of the sentence – 'I gave him all the money' and 'I earned' – are linked together by the relative pronoun 'that'.
- A negative is a word like 'not' or 'never' that indicates an action is not being done.
- Gender refers to whether a word is masculine or feminine.
- The subject is the name given to the person or thing doing the action. In the sentence above, the subject is 'the girl'.

- The direct object is the name given to the person or thing that has the action done directly to it. In the sentence on the previous page, 'a cake' is the object because it is made by the girl.

PROGRESS CHECK

1. Read this sentence and answer the following questions:
   The clumsy goalkeeper suddenly dropped the ball.
   (a) What is the subject?
   (b) Find the verb.
   (c) Find an adjective.
   (d) Find an adverb.
   (e) Find a definite article.
2. Read this sentence and answer the following questions:
   He dropped it at my feet and I scored.
   (a) Find an object pronoun.
   (b) Find a preposition.
   (c) Find a noun.
   (d) Find a conjunction.

1. (a) goalkeeper
   (b) dropped
   (c) clumsy
   (d) suddenly
   (e) the
2. (a) it
   (b) at
   (c) feet
   (d) and

The indefinite article

AQA	✓
OCR	✓
EDEXCEL	✓
WJEC	✓
CCEA	✓

The indefinite article is the grammatical way of referring to 'a' or 'an'. In French, the indefinite article is **un** or **une**:

- Use **un** before a masculine noun.
- Use **une** before a feminine noun.
- 'To a' is **à un** or **à une**, e.g.:

  to a match   **à un match**
  to a school   **à une école**
- 'Of a' is **d'un** or **d'une**, e.g.:

  the roof of a castle   **le toit d'un château**
  the roof of a house   **le toit d'une maison**

KEY POINT

Leave out **un** and **une** when stating a person's job, e.g.:
He is a teacher.   **Il est professeur**.

PROGRESS CHECK

Say or write the following in French:
1. I go to a match.
2. The roof of a castle
3. He is a teacher.

1. Je vais à un match.
2. Le toit d'un château
3. Il est professeur.

The definite article

AQA	✓
OCR	✓
EDEXCEL	✓
WJEC	✓
CCEA	✓

The definite article is the grammatical way of referring to 'the'. In French, the definite article is **le** (before a masculine singular noun), **la** (before a feminine singular noun), **l'** (before a noun that starts with a vowel or silent 'h') or **les** (before a plural noun).

Look at the four ways of saying 'to the':

- **Au** is used before masculine singular nouns, e.g.:

    Je vais au cinéma.   I am going to the cinema.

- **À la** is used before feminine singular nouns, e.g.:

    Je vais à la mairie.   I am going to the town hall.

- **À l'** is used before singular nouns beginning with a vowel or silent 'h', e.g.:

    Je vais à l'université.   I am going to the university.

- **Aux** is used before all plural nouns, e.g.:

    Je vais aux États-Unis.   I am going to the USA.

Look at the four ways of saying 'of the':

- **Du** is used before masculine singular nouns, e.g.:

    la fille du professeur   the teacher's daughter

- **De la** is used before feminine singular nouns, e.g.:

    le fils de la secrétaire   the secretary's son

- **De l'** is used before singular nouns beginning with a vowel or silent 'h', e.g.:

    le chapeau de l'homme   the man's hat

- **Des** is used before all plural nouns, e.g.:

    les parents des jeunes   the young people's parents

PROGRESS CHECK

Say or write the following in French:
1. The man's car
2. The teacher's hat
3. I am going to the school.
4. I am going to the gym.

1. La voiture de l'homme
2. Le chapeau du professeur
3. Je vais à l'école.
4. Je vais au gymnase.

The partitive article

AQA ✓
OCR ✓
EDEXCEL ✓
WJEC ✓
CCEA ✓

The partitive article is the grammatical way of referring to 'some'/'any':

- **Du** is used before masculine singular nouns, e.g.:

    du vin   some wine

- **De la** is used before feminine singular nouns, e.g.:

    de la farine   some flour

- **De l'** is used before singular nouns beginning with a vowel or silent 'h', e.g.:

    de l'eau   some water

- **Des** is used before all plural nouns, e.g.:

    des amis   some friends

PROGRESS CHECK

Say or write the following in French:
1. Some bottles
2. Some jam
3. Some bread
4. Some meat

1. Des bouteilles
2. De la confiture
3. Du pain
4. De la viande

Sample controlled assessment

Speaking

1 You are going to have a conversation with your teacher about the pictures below.

Le départ

Le transport

L'arrivée

Pendant le voyage

La maison

Avant le match

Après le match

Pendant le match

Examiner's comments

Your teacher can choose any title or format for your controlled speaking assessment. Your teacher might give you a series of pictures to describe, such as the ones opposite about a football trip to France that did not go quite to plan. A model conversation is given on page 23.

Your speaking assessment will last between four and six minutes. That is a long time. It means you will have to give plenty of detail to fill the time.

Sample controlled assessment

Student: Enfin la grande aventure allait[13] commencer. Toute l'équipe s'est rassemblée[11] de très bon matin[16] et on est parti d'Angleterre - de devant le collège - à six heures du matin en car, et après un long voyage on est arrivé très fatigué à seize heures, et mon correspondant m'attendait[13/32] au collège. Pendant le voyage, j'ai lu et j'ai écouté de la musique. Tout de suite,[16] en arrivant,[7] nous sommes allés chez lui en voiture. Son père conduisait. Sa maison était petite mais confortable. Il y avait un petit jardin charmant avec des fleurs et une pelouse. C'était comme un jardin britannique typique, mais pas aussi beau.[22]

Teacher: Tu avais faim?

Student: Oui, j'ai mangé un sandwich au jambon et j'ai bu un verre de limonade. Après avoir dormi[8] un peu, nous sommes sortis pour nous entraîner.[31] Nous avons fait de l'exercice et nous avons pratiqué avec le ballon. Puis on est rentré et j'ai passé la soirée à regarder[16] la télé et à causer avec mon correspondant. Plus tard, on est allé à un café pour boire[31] un verre de limonade et pour causer[31] avec nos amis français. L'ambiance était géniale.[15] Le lendemain, mon correspondant a retrouvé ses amis. Il faisait beau et le soleil brillait. Il faisait vraiment[18] trop chaud pour un match de football. On est allé au stade municipal pour le grand match. À trois heures de l'après-midi, le match a commencé. À la mi-temps, l'équipe britannique menait 2-0, et moi, j'avais marqué[17] un des buts d'un coup franc. Mais juste après la mi-temps, quel désastre![9] Je me suis blessé.

Teacher: Qu'est-ce qui s'est passé?

Student: Un des joueurs français était fâché parce que[2] son équipe perdait et son tackle a été très violent. Je me suis cassé la jambe. La douleur était incroyable.[16] Mes copains n'étaient pas contents non plus. Mon professeur a appelé une ambulance et elle est arrivée dix minutes plus tard. Je suis resté trois jours à l'hôpital et mes amis sont venus me[32] voir tous les jours. L'hôpital était très agréable et les infirmières m'ont[32] très bien soigné.

Teacher: Tes collègues t'ont apporté des cadeaux?

Student: Oui, ils m'ont[32] apporté des fruits, du chocolat et des livres. Toute l'équipe française est venue me voir. Le joueur violent m'a présenté ses excuses. Comme cadeau, il m'a donné une montre en or. Ses parents ont écrit à mes parents pour s'excuser.[31] Je pense que ma visite en France a été un désastre et que je n'y retournerai[12] jamais.[24]

Turn to page 155 for a translation of this passage.

Examiner's comments

This student has incorporated a number of the '32 points for improving your grade' from pages 8–10 and is on track for a top grade:

2 'Parce que'
7 'En' + the present participle
8 'Après avoir' + the past participle
9 An exclamation
11 An example of the perfect tense
12 A future tense has been included
13 Examples of the imperfect tense
15 An example of an adjective
16 Impressive vocabulary and structures, e.g. 'de très bon matin', 'tout de suite', 'j'ai passé la soirée à regarder', 'incroyable'
17 An example of a pluperfect
18 'Vraiment' has been used
22 An example of a comparative
24 A negative has been used
31 Examples of 'pour' + the infinitive
32 Pronouns have been used

Sample controlled assessment

Writing

1 Write an imaginary magazine interview with a French-speaking celebrity tennis player, addressing the following points:

- Introduce the person to the reader
- His/her early career
- His/her family
- Keeping fit
- Leisure interests
- Views on the world today.

Interview avec Isabelle Frétey – vedette internationale

Tout le monde a entendu parler d'Isabelle: la meilleure joueuse[23] de tennis en France. Déjà à l'âge de 24 ans elle avait gagné[17] trois tournois et cet été elle va essayer[12] de gagner le tournoi de Wimbledon. Parisienne, belle, elle est vraiment vedette. Mais sa vie n'a pas toujours été si facile.

Isabelle, raconte-nous ta jeunesse.

La vie était dure. Quel cauchemar![9] Mes parents sont morts quand j'avais trois ans[13] et je suis allée vivre avec ma tante dans un faubourg difficile de Paris. Il n'y avait pas de courts de tennis. Pour jouer[31] je devais faire un trajet d'une heure en métro. Mais enfin j'ai trouvé un bon club. J'étais membre depuis[26] un an quand j'ai fait la connaissance de Marcel qui est maintenant mon entraîneur et mon mari.

Et que fais-tu pour rester en bonne condition physique?

L'important est de bien manger.[16] Je ne bois jamais[24] d'alcool, je ne fume pas et je fais de l'exercice. Et je joue au tennis avec Marcel quatre heures par jour.

Et ton premier triomphe?

J'ai gagné mon premier tournoi aux États-Unis. J'étais si contente. Après avoir gagné,[8] nous avons fêté notre triomphe avec un repas dans un restaurant cinq étoiles.

À part le tennis, qu'est-ce que tu aimes faire?

J'adore la lecture. En rentrant[7] chez moi, ce qui me plaît c'est de m'installer dans un fauteuil et de lire un roman.

Et ta famille?

Je suis fille unique et ma tante est morte. Mais j'ai Marcel, mon mari, et un jour on espère avoir des enfants. Mais avant d'avoir[6] des enfants, j'ai envie de[1] gagner encore des tournois. Il faut que j'aille[25] à Wimbledon et il faut que je gagne.

Et les problèmes du monde?

Pour moi, le problème principal[15] est l'environnement. Le monde ne fait pas assez d'attention à ce qui se passe. On est en train de détruire la planète.[3]

Isabelle, bonne chance à Wimbledon.

Merci.

Turn to page 155 for a translation of this passage.

Examiner's comments

Remember that you will have to write two controlled assessments, each of up to 300 words. Here is a good example that uses a number of the '32 points for improving your grade' from pages 8–10:

1 An 'avoir' structure
3 A point of view
6 An 'avant de' structure
7 'En' + the present participle
8 'Après avoir' + the past participle
9 An exclamation
12 An example of a future tense
13 An imperfect tense has been used here
15 This is just one example of an adjective in this piece
16 An impressive structure
17 A pluperfect has been used
23 An example of a superlative
24 A negative has been included
25 Extra marks for including a subjunctive
26 'Depuis'
31 'Pour' + the infinitive

Sample controlled assessment

2 Write an e-mail from a hospital ward, telling your friend about an imaginary accident you had. You could mention...

- what you were doing before the accident happened
- the weather at the time
- what exactly happened
- someone who helped you
- how you got to hospital
- the outcome.

Chère Madeleine,

Je suis à l'hôpital! J'ai fait une promenade à la campagne. Il pleuvait et je suis tombée. Je me suis cassé la jambe et le bras. Mon ami a appelé une ambulance. Elle est arrivée cinq minutes plus tard. Ici à l'hôpital, j'ai lu deux livres et j'ai écouté de la musique. Les infirmières sont aimables et la nourriture est bonne. Hier, j'ai mangé un steak frites et j'ai bu du vin! Je suis contente ici. Je vais sortir de l'hôpital demain.

A bientôt, Paula

Now compare the version above with the one below.

Chère Madeleine,

Je suis à l'hôpital depuis[26] deux jours. Il y a trois jours[16], comme il faisait beau, j'ai décidé de[4] faire une longue[15] promenade à la campagne près de chez moi. Mon frère aîné[15] m'a[32] accompagnée.

Tout d'un coup,[16] le temps a changé. Un orage! Il a commencé à pleuvoir.[16] Bientôt,[16] il pleuvait à verse et j'étais trempée jusqu'aux os.[16] Et j'avais froid[1] aussi. Quel désastre![9] En essayant[7] de rentrer le plus vite possible,[23] malheureusement[16] j'ai glissé dans la boue et je suis tombée. Quelle horreur![9] Je me suis cassé la jambe et le bras. La douleur était terrible! Sans perdre de temps[5], mon frère a appelé une ambulance. Après avoir téléphoné,[8] mon frère m'a[32] donné son pardessus et j'avais moins froid. Sans lui, je serais[14] morte. L'ambulance est arrivée cinq minutes plus tard[16] et j'ai raconté aux ambulanciers ce qui était arrivé.[17] Dix minutes plus tard, j'étais arrivée[17] à l'hôpital.

Ici à l'hôpital, j'ai déjà[16] lu deux livres et j'écoute de la musique. Les infirmières sont aimables et la nourriture est bonne. On me[32] donne tout ce que je demande. Je pense que les hôpitaux en France sont les meilleurs du monde parce que la cuisine est si bonne et les médecins ont toujours le temps de faire ce qu'il faut, tandis qu'en[30] Angleterre les médecins semblent toujours si pressés.[3] Je peux choisir ce que je veux. Hier, j'ai mangé un steak frites et j'ai même[16] bu du vin! Je suis contente parce que[2] je vais sortir[12] de l'hôpital demain. Tout est bien qui finit bien.[16] Mais je ne ferai plus[24] de promenades à la campagne. Il faut que je fasse[25] mes promenades dans le parc.

A bientôt, Paula

Turn to page 155 for a translation of this passage.

Examiner's comments

The first example is very short and is of grade D standard. If you want a high grade, though, you should aim for about 300 words as in the second example. The numbers in the text once again refer to the '32 points for improving your grade' on pages 8–10:

1 An 'avoir' structure

2 'Parce que'

3 An extended point of view with a justification

4 'J'ai décidé de...'

5 'Sans' + the infinitive

7 'En' + the present participle

8 'Après avoir' + the past participle

9 Exclamations

12 A future tense has been used here

14 An example of a conditional

15 Nice adjectives

16 Impressive vocabulary and structures, including adverbial/time expressions, weather descriptions and a proverb ('tout est bien qui finit bien')

17 Examples of pluperfects

23 A superlative is used here

24 A good example of a negative

25 A mark-winning subjunctive

26 A 'depuis' structure

30 'Tandis que' is a good connective

32 Personal pronouns always get you extra marks

Exam practice questions

Listening

1 **TRACK 3** Listen to this conversation between Jean and Edgar. Tick the correct boxes as required.

(a) Why doesn't Jean go to Greece?

   A He doesn't like Greece. ☐

   B He has no money. ☐

   C He doesn't have time. ☐

(b) What is Jean's girlfriend doing?

   A She is going away on holiday. ☐

   B She is looking for a job. ☐

   C She is staying in Lyon. ☐

(c) What does Jean say about Lyon?

   A He finds the city boring. ☐

   B He loves the city. ☐

   C He hates the city. ☐

(d) Where will Jean work?

   A In a factory ☐   **B** In a garden ☐   **C** In a school ☐

(e) As well as earning money, how will the work benefit Jean?

....

(f) What will Jean do in the evening?

   A Play cards ☐   **B** Go to the cinema ☐   **C** Watch TV ☐

(g) Why doesn't Jean go to Spain?

   A He hates Spain. ☐

   B He doesn't have any money. ☐

   C The holidays aren't long enough. ☐

(h) How did Jean get to Spain last year?

   A By train ☐   **B** By plane ☐   **C** By hitch-hiking ☐

(i) What food and drink did Jean enjoy in Spain?

   A Chicken and wine ☐   **B** Sausages and beer ☐   **C** Cake and coffee ☐   **(9)**

Exam practice questions

2 TRACK 4 What are the customers ordering to eat and drink? Tick the two correct boxes for each customer.

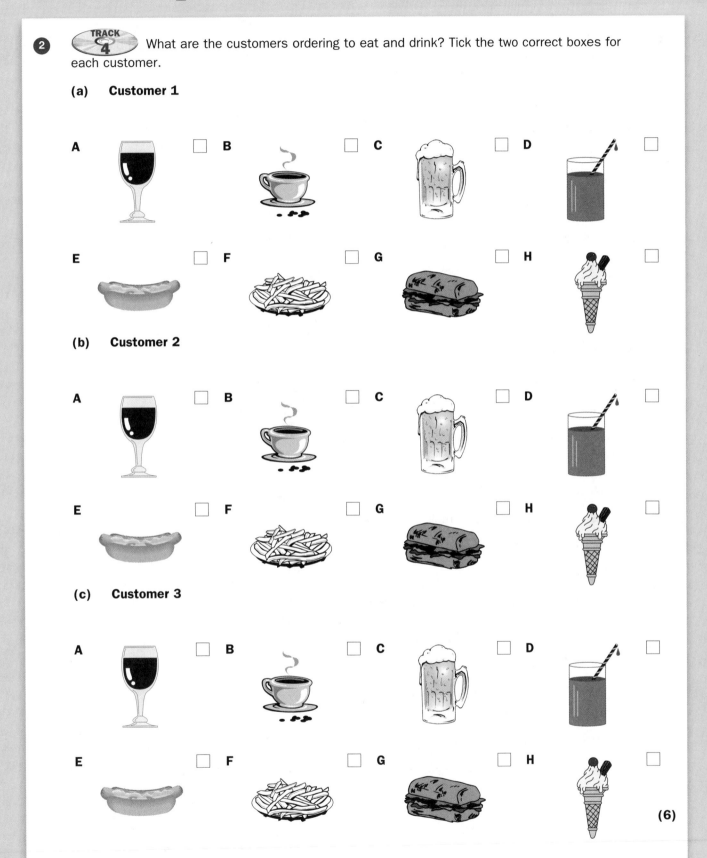

(a) **Customer 1**

(b) **Customer 2**

(c) **Customer 3**

(6)

Exam practice questions

3 **TRACK 5** Listen to the man talking about how his life has changed. Tick the correct boxes.

(a) How many kilos in weight has the man lost?

A 10 ☐ **B** 20 ☐ **C** 30 ☐

(b) How did he lose weight?

A He stopped smoking. ☐

B He did a lot of exercise. ☐

C He played badminton. ☐

(c) Why did he start smoking?

A To look good with the girls. ☐

B To put on weight. ☐

C There was no particular reason, it was almost by chance. ☐

(d) How many cigarettes did he smoke?

A One a day ☐

B A packet a day ☐

C About 40 a day ☐

(e) Why did he stop smoking?

A His girlfriend did not like it. ☐

B It might have made him ill. ☐

C It was expensive. ☐

(f) How quickly did he stop?

A Immediately ☐ **B** In two days ☐ **C** In a few days ☐

(g) What did Anne do when he smoked?

A She kept her distance. ☐

B She smoked as well. ☐

C She bought him cigarettes. ☐

(h) What does Anne do now?

A She has given up smoking. ☐

B She sits beside him. ☐

C She keeps her distance. ☐

(8)

Exam practice questions

4 **TRACK 6** Listen to the conversation between Elise and Pierre. Tick the correct boxes.

(a) Where is Elise sore?

    A Head ☐   **B** Leg ☐   **C** Back ☐

(b) What caused her illness?

    A The sun ☐   **B** Food ☐   **C** Stress ☐

(c) How often has Elise been ill recently?

    A Never ☐   **B** It is the second time ☐   **C** Often ☐

(d) Where is Elise going?

    A Bed ☐   **B** Cinema ☐   **C** Concert ☐

(e) What is Pierre's attitude?

    A He is happy. ☐

    B He does not believe her. ☐

    C He does not want to go out. ☐

(f) What does Elise ask for?

    A A kiss ☐

    B Money ☐

    C Permission ☐   **(6)**

Reading

1 Read the information and answer the questions that follow about who likes what.

JEAN-PAUL	J'aime tous les fruits mais je préfère les pêches.
MONIQUE	J'aime tous les fruits mais je préfère les cerises.
ESTELLE	J'aime tous les fruits mais je préfère les citrons.
LUC	J'aime toutes les viandes mais je préfère l'agneau.
EDGAR	J'aime toutes les viandes mais je préfère le canard.
ANNE	J'aime toutes les viandes mais je préfère le veau.
MARIE	J'aime tous les légumes mais je préfère les petis pois.
BERNADETTE	J'aime tous les légumes mais je préfère les champignons.
CLAUDE	J'aime tous les légumes mais je préfère les haricots verts.
PIERRE	J'adore la confiture.
ROSE	J'adore les œufs.

Exam practice questions

(a) Who likes eggs? ....

(b) Who likes lamb? ....

(c) Who likes duck? ....

(d) Who likes French beans? ....

(e) Who likes mushrooms? ....

(f) Who likes peas? ....

(g) Who likes veal? ....

(h) Who likes peaches? ....

(i) Who likes lemons? ....

(j) Who likes cherries? ....

(k) Who likes jam? ....   **(11)**

2 Match the people to the statements. You will have to use names more than once.

MONIQUE	Tous mes amis adorent les hamburgers mais moi non. Pour moi, les fruits et les légumes. Je ne mange pas de viande. Mes parents disent que je ne mange pas assez mais je surveille ma ligne!
PIERRE	J'aime bien les hamburgers et j'en mange tout le temps surtout quand je travaille. Les légumes et les fruits ne me disent rien. Mes parents essayent de me faire manger les choses saines mais je refuse.
JACQUES	Les Français mangent tout le temps. Ils parlent tout le temps de cuisine. Moi, je mange pour vivre pas le contraire.
ANNE	J'adore le fast-food et j'adore faire un McDo. Ailleurs c'est trop cher.

(a) I am concerned about my figure. ....

(b) I cannot afford restaurants. ....

(c) I insist on eating unhealthily. ....

(d) I think the French are obsessed with food. ....

(e) I am a vegetarian. ....

(f) I try to eat healthily. ....

(g) I love fast-food. ....

(h) I do not like fast-food. ....

(i) I am told I do not eat enough. ....   **(9)**

Exam practice questions

3 Read these adverts and answer the questions that follow.

A

Restaurant Italien
La chaleur de l'accueil italien

Le restaurant est ouvert tous les jours
du mardi au dimanche

Formule du midi à 10 euros

B

Restaurant Chez Monique

Specialités portugaises	Specialités:
Produits à emporter	Lundi: Morue au four
Menu du midi à 11 euros	Mardi: Crevettes
	Mercredi: Huîtres fraîches

Renseignez-vous!

C

Restaurant Descartes
à deux pas de l'hôtel de ville

MIDI plat à 12 euros
Ouvert du lundi au samedi
Le dimanche sur réservation
Venez danser au rythme de la musique latine.

(a) Write the letter of the restaurant that has the cheapest lunchtime menu. ....

(b) Write the letter of the restaurant that is closed on Mondays. ....

(c) What is being served at restaurant B on Mondays? ....

(d) What is being served at restaurant B on Tuesdays? ....

(e) What is being served at restaurant B on Wednesdays? ....

(f) Write the letter of the restaurant that is near the town hall. ....

(g) Write the letter of the restaurant that is normally closed on Sundays. ....

(h) What must you do if you want to eat at restaurant C on Sundays? ....

(i) Write the letter of the restaurant that offers take-away food. .... **(9)**

4 Read this text message and answer the questions that follow.

> Désolée mais je ne peux pas aller à la patinoire ce soir. J'ai mal à la gorge. Je pense que c'est la grippe. Je vais rester au lit. Ma mère m'a donné des pastilles pour la gorge et demain je vais chez le médecin. Demande à Pierre s'il veut y aller.

(a) Where were they going? ....

(b) What is the problem? ....

(c) What is causing the problem? ....

(d) How will she spend the evening? ....

(e) What did her mother give her? ....

(f) Where is she going tomorrow? ....

(g) What does she suggest? .... **(7)**

Exam practice questions

5 Read this e-mail. Answer the questions that follow, ticking the correct boxes where required.

Salut!

Comment vas-tu? Moi, je vais bien. Excuse-moi de ne pas t'avoir contacté plus tôt, mais en ce moment je suis débordée! D'abord, il y avait la rentrée des classes et il a fallu que je me remette au rythme de l'école! (Tous les jours je me lève à six heures et je ne rentre qu'à six ou sept heures du soir – cela dépend des jours. Je t'envoie mon emploi de temps.)

J'espère que tu as passé de bonnes vacances d'été. Pour moi, c'était désastreux! On m'a opéré des dents de sagesse – on m'a enlevé les quatre dents. Je suis restée trois jours à l'hôpital et ensuite je ne devais ni sortir ni prendre le soleil. Je ne pouvais pas non plus me baigner dans la piscine – et il faisait tellement chaud!

Je te remercie pour les photos ... Adele

(a) Why has Adele not been in contact?

    A She has been overworked. ☐

    B She forgot. ☐

    C She has been ill. ☐   **(1)**

(b) What has happened recently?

    A Christmas ☐   **B** Return to school ☐   **C** A wedding ☐   **(1)**

(c) What does Adele feel she has to do?

    A Get used to school rhythm. ☐

    B Work harder. ☐

    C Contact her teachers. ☐   **(1)**

(d) Adele thinks her day is too…

    A short ☐   **B** long ☐   **C** easy ☐   **(1)**

(e) What is Adele sending?

    A Her timetable ☐   **B** Her photos ☐   **C** Her new number ☐   **(1)**

(f) What has Adele lost?

    A Her purse ☐   **B** Her patience ☐   **C** Her wisdom teeth ☐   **(1)**

(g) What three things was she unable to do?

    (i) ....

    (ii) ....

    (iii) ....   **(3)**

Exam practice questions

6 Read this article on travel sickness.

> **Vous partez en vacances en voiture?**
> **Onze manières d'éviter le mal de la route.**
> - Achetez un médicament contre le mal de la route. Prenez-le la veille de votre départ.
> - Allez au lit de bonne heure la veille de votre départ.
> - Ne fumez pas pendant le voyage.
> - Demandez aux autres passagers de ne pas fumer.
> - Ne mangez pas un grand repas avant le départ. Mais il ne faut pas avoir l'estomac vide.
> - Ne mangez rien pendant le voyage.
> - Dans la voiture, mettez-vous à côté du chauffeur.
> - Essayez de parler tout le temps avec les autres passagers.
> - Ne lisez pas pendant le voyage.
> - Si possible, laissez une vitre ouverte.
> - Pendant les arrêts, promenez-vous en plein air.

Complete the sentences below by choosing the correct words from the options given in this box.

faites	devant	lit	s'arrêter	médicaments	fermées
causer		couchez	cigarettes	peu	enfant

Le jour d'avant

Prenez vos **(a)** .... et **(b)** .... -vous de bonne heure.

Le chauffeur

Demandez au chauffeur si vous pouvez vous mettre **(c)** ....

Demandez-lui aussi de **(d)** .... de temps en temps.

Pendant le voyage

Avant de partir, mangez un **(e)** .... Evitez les **(f)** ....

et demandez aux autres passagers de **(g)** .... avec vous.

Dites-leur que vous ne voulez pas avoir les vitres **(h)** ....

Pendant les arrêts, **(i)** .... des promenades. **(9)**

Exam practice questions

7 Read this article about an actor called Alex Martyn and answer the questions that follow.

ALEX MARTYN "La chose la plus importante dans la vie, c'est la santé!"

Vous adorez Alex Martyn? Réjouissez-vous! Il est en bonne condition physique. Il court 5 kilomètres par jour. Quant à son prochain rôle, ce sera celui d'un détective privé à la poursuite d'un serial killer.

Enfance
Né à Salem, dans l'Oregon, le 29 juin 1966, Alex Edward Martyn mesure 1,85m pour 73kg. Il a un frère, Michael, et une sœur, Rachel. Son père, George, dirige une société de transports routiers, et sa maman, Mary, est infirmière. De confession baptiste, ses parents lui ont inculqué des principes religieux assez stricts, dont il dit aujourd'hui qu'ils sont «ses meilleurs guides dans la vie».

Personnalité
Anxieux et manquant d'assurance, il se définit lui-même comme tel: «Je suis mal à l'aise».

Études
Alors qu'il est inscrit à l'université du Kansas en journalisme, option publicité, et qu'il est à deux doigts d'obtenir son diplôme, Alex Martyn plie bagage, range toutes ses affaires dans sa Ford et prend la route, direction la Californie, sous le prétexte de poursuivre ses études dans une école d'arts graphiques à Pasadena. En réalité, il s'inscrit à des cours de comédie, exerçant différents jobs pour survivre.

Aversion
Alex déteste cuisiner! Il dit: «C'est une perte de temps et je ne suis pas bon en cuisine. Je préfère manger dans un bon restaurant où un chef prépare un repas délicieux.»

Loisirs
Promener ses chiens en laisse, jouer du violon, écouter de la musique ou encore partir avec sa voiture camper en pleine nature font partie de ses loisirs favoris. Tout cela l'aidant, comme il le dit à «garder la tête froide.»

(a) What is the most important thing in life according to Alex? .... **(1)**

(b) What does Alex do to keep fit? .... **(1)**

(c) What is his next film role? .... **(1)**

(d) In which US state was he born? .... **(1)**

(e) What kind of firm does Alex's father have? .... **(1)**

(f) What does his mother do for a living? .... **(1)**

(g) What are his best guides through life? .... **(1)**

(h) In Alex's personality, what does he lack? .... **(1)**

(i) What career was he initially interested in? .... **(1)**

(j) What does Alex hate doing? .... **(1)**

(k) How does he spend his leisure time? List four activities.

    (i) ....

    (ii) ....

    (iii) ....

    (iv) .... **(4)**

Exam practice questions

8 Read this e-mail and answer the questions that follow.

> Salut Michael.
>
> Tu me demandes ce que je fais pour être en forme. Alors, je joue au hockey et fais de longues promenades avec le chien. Comme ça je reste assez mince.
>
> J'ai deux petites sœurs qui sont pénibles. Mon père est agriculteur et on habite dans une ferme. J'ai ma propre chambre et quand tu viendras, tu auras une chambre au rez-de-chaussée. Pendant ton séjour mes sœurs vont partager une chambre et ça les embête!
>
> Ah! Mes sœurs! Quand je regarde la télé, elles veulent toujours regarder l'autre chaîne. Dans ce cas-là je me renferme dans ma chambre pour lire.
>
> Je ne fume pas et je ne bois pas d'alcool. Et toi?
>
> Georges

(a) What does Georges do to keep fit? Name two activities.

   (i) ....

   (ii) .... **(2)**

(b) How would you describe Georges's figure?

.... **(1)**

(c) What problem does Georges have?

.... **(1)**

(d) What does Georges's father do?

.... **(1)**

(e) Where will Michael's bedroom be?

.... **(1)**

(f) What will annoy Georges's sisters?

.... **(1)**

(g) How do Georges's sisters annoy him?

.... **(1)**

(h) Where does Georges take refuge?

.... **(1)**

(i) Name two things that Georges does not do.

   (i) .... **(ii)** .... **(2)**

Exam practice questions

9 Read this e-mail from your penfriend Claire about a weekend spent shopping and **answer the questions**.

Salut!

J'ai vécu une journée formidable aujourd'hui! J'ai fait des courses avec ma meilleure amie Martine.

Je me suis levée assez tôt à sept heures moins le quart et nous avons quitté la maison vers huit heures. Pour le petit déjeuner j'ai pris un croissant avec de la confiture et j'ai bu du chocolat chaud. Je sais que je suis teenager mais je n'aime pas le café!

D'habitude, nous allons en auto mais aujourd'hui nous sommes arrivées en ville en car et sommes allées tout de suite dans un grand magasin où j'ai acheté des chaussures. Après ça nous sommes allées dans un petit magasin de mode où j'ai acheté une belle jupe bleue. J'ai payé seulement dix euros au lieu de vingt euros – un rabais de 50% - parce que c'était en solde – pas mal quoi!

Comme il pleuvait nous avons décidé d'aller au cinéma et nous avons vu « Le printemps des poètes » un film d'amour. Moi, j'ai bien aimé le film mais Martine n'était pas d'accord. D'habitude, elle préfère les films à suspense!

Pour rentrer à la maison nous avons pris le train – un bon choix parce que nous avons vu de grands embouteillages sur la route principale.

A bientôt.
Claire

Example: What sort of day has Claire had? *Fantastic*

(a) How long did it take Claire to get ready to go out? ....

(b) What did she eat for breakfast? ....

(c) What did she drink for breakfast? ....

(d) How did Claire and Martine travel to town? ....

(e) Why did her skirt cost only 10 euros? ....

(f) Why did they decide to go to the cinema? ....

(g) What did Martine think of the film? ....

(h) Why was Claire glad they took the train home? .... **(8)**

WJEC Foundation Tier

2 Relationships and choices

The following topics are covered in this chapter:

- **Relationships with family and friends**
- **Future plans regarding marriage or partnership**
- **Social issues**
- **Equality**
- **Grammar**

2.1 Relationships with family and friends

LEARNING SUMMARY	After studying this section, you should be able to:
	• talk about your family, friends and pets
	• describe your relationships with people

Relationships with family and friends

AQA	✓
OCR	✓
EDEXCEL	✓
WJEC	✓
CCEA	✓

You will find the following vocabulary and sentences useful for the reading and listening exams. You might carry out a controlled assessment on relationships with family and friends in either speaking or writing.

Family

le père · la grand-mère · la mère · le grand-père · la sœur · le frère

la dame

enceinte

Self and family (Toi-même et ta famille)

aîné(e) – older, oldest
l'amour (m) – love
le beau-frère – brother-in-law
le beau-père – stepfather, father-in-law
le bébé – baby
la belle-mère – stepmother, mother-in-law
la belle-sœur – sister-in-law
cadet(te) – younger, youngest
célibataire – single (not married)
la cohabitation – living together
le cousin/la cousine – cousin
la dame – lady
le demi-frère – half-brother
la demi-sœur – half-sister
la dispute – argument
le divorce – divorce
enceinte – pregnant
l'enfant (m/f) – child
l'épouse (f) – wife
l'époux (m) – husband
la famille monoparentale – single-parent family
la femme – wife, woman
le/la fiancé(e) – fiancé(e)
la fille – girl, daughter
le fils – son
le foyer – home
le frère – brother
le/la gosse – child, kid
la grand-mère – grandmother
les grands-parents (m, pl) – grandparents
le grand-père – grandfather

l'homme (m) – man
le jumeau/la jumelle – twin
les liens de parenté (m, pl) – family, blood ties
la maison familiale – family home
maman – mum
le mari – husband
le mariage – wedding, marriage
les membres de la famille (m, pl) – family members
la mère – mother
la mère célibataire – single mother
naître – to be born
le neveu – nephew
la nièce – niece
l'oncle (m) – uncle
papa – dad
les parents (m, pl) – parents
le/la partenaire – partner
le père – father
le père célibataire – single father
le petit ami/la petite amie – boyfriend/girlfriend
les petits-enfants (m, pl) – grandchildren
la petite-fille – granddaughter
le petit-fils – grandson
les rapports (m, pl) – relationship
les relations (f, pl) – relationship
la séparation – separation
la sœur – sister
la tante – aunt
le veuf – widower
la veuve – widow

KEY POINT

Note the two meanings of **le mariage**.

l'invitation

Friends and guests (Les amis et les invités)

l'ami (m), l'amie (f) – friend
la bise – kiss (on cheek)
la boum – party
le/la camarade – friend
le/la copain (-ine) – friend
le/la correspondant(e) – penfriend
l'hospitalité (f) – hospitality
l'invitation (f) – invitation

le jumelage – twinning
jumelé(e) – twinned
la lettre – letter
le rendez-vous – meeting, appointment
la réponse – reply
la ville jumelée – twin town
les vœux (m, pl) – wishes

Pets (Les animaux de compagnie)

le chat – cat

le chien – dog

le cobaye – guinea pig

le cochon d'Inde – guinea pig

le hamster – hamster

le perroquet – parrot

la perruche – budgerigar

le poisson rouge – goldfish

Verbs

danser

accompagner – to accompany

aimer bien – to quite like

s'amuser – to have a good time

chanter – to sing

cohabiter – to live together

correspondre – to correspond

danser – to dance

disputer – to argue

divorcer d'avec – to divorce

s'écrire – to write to each other

s'entendre avec – to get on well with

épouser – to marry

faire des promenades – to go for walks

faire du babysitting – to babysit

faire la connaissance – to get to know

inviter – to invite

prendre des photos – to take photos

présenter – to introduce

recevoir – to receive

se rencontrer – to meet

rendre visite à – to visit (a person)

rester au foyer – to stay at home

se séparer de – to separate from

se voir – to see each other

voir – to see

PROGRESS CHECK

Say or write the following in French:

1. I have a nephew and two nieces.
2. I have a goldfish and a hamster.
3. I went to the cinema with my family.

1. J'ai un neveu et deux nièces.
2. J'ai un poisson rouge et un hamster.
3. Je suis allé(e) au cinéma avec ma famille.

Controlled speaking assessment: you and your family

Make sure you can answer these questions without thinking. Get someone to ask you the questions so you can practise answering them without using the book.

Tu t'appelles comment?
Je m'appelle ....

Tu as quel âge?
J'ai .... ans.

Il y a combien de personnes dans ta famille?
Il y a .... personnes.

Qui sont-ils?
Il y a mon père, ma mère, mon frère, ma sœur et moi.

Et ton père, qu'est-ce qu'il fait dans la vie?
Il est ....[1]

Et ta mère, qu'est-ce qu'elle fait dans la vie?
Elle est ....

Tu es né(e)[2] en quelle année?
Je suis né(e) en mille neuf cent quatre-vingt-seize.

Où es-tu né(e)?
Je suis né(e) à ....

Tu fais quelle taille?[3]
Je fais un mètre soixante-dix.

Tu as des animaux à la maison?
J'ai un chien et un chat.

Tu as un/une meilleur(e) ami(e)?
Oui, il/elle s'appelle ....

C'est quand, ton anniversaire?
C'est le ....

1. Note that in French you don't say 'un(e)' when stating someone's job. You have to say, for example, 'He/She is teacher'.

2. Use 'né' for boys, 'née' for girls.

3. 'Taille' means size: How tall are you?

> **KEY POINT**
>
> You will be assessed on your communication skills and also on your quality of language. You will be asked to show your knowledge of tenses.

Follow these tips when preparing for the controlled speaking assessment:

- Try to use impressive vocabulary: make your own private list of out-of-the-ordinary words.
- Try to put expression into what you say.
- Your answers should not be a pre-learnt speech. However, you must be able to talk for between four and six minutes on each topic.
- Why not record your answers and listen to them whenever you can?

1 Don't just stop here. Add more information!

2 You have used a present tense (see pages 50–54). Just a perfect and a future to go!

3 This means 'what is she like?'

4 The more kinds of relatives you add, the more marks you get.

5 You have given an opinion and are justifying it. This gets extra marks.

6 You have used a perfect tense (see pages 92–93) and a future tense (see page 120). You are on course for at least a grade C.

🗨 **Décris ta famille.**

🗨 **On est cinq, mon père, ma mère, mon frère, ma sœur et moi.[1] On a un chat. Mon père travaille dans une usine.[2] Je ne sais pas exactement ce qu'il fait. Ma mère est professeur.**

🗨 **Et ta mère, comment est-elle?[3]**

🗨 **Elle est assez grande et elle a les yeux bleus. Elle a cinquante ans et elle aime regarder la télé.**

🗨 **Il y a d'autres membres de ta famille?**

🗨 **J'ai un grand-père, une grand-mère, deux oncles, trois tantes, un cousin, deux cousines.[4] Je vois mes grands-parents tous les week-ends.**

🗨 **Quel est ton animal préféré?**

🗨 **J'adore les chiens.**

🗨 **Pourquoi?**

🗨 **Ils sont affectueux.[5]**

🗨 **Pour ton anniversaire, quels cadeaux as-tu reçu?**

🗨 **J'ai reçu[6] de l'argent, des livres, des vêtements et des CD.**

🗨 **Qu'est-ce que tu feras avec l'argent?**

🗨 **J'achèterai[6] encore des vêtements.**

Other useful sentences

La vie familiale en Grande-Bretagne.
Family life in Great Britain.

Chaque jour en Grande-Bretagne, 800 couples se marient, 300 couples divorcent et 3000 enfants naissent.
Every day in Great Britain, 800 couples get married, 300 couples get divorced and 3000 children are born.

Le nombre de célibataires augmente.
The number of single people is increasing.

Célibataires, retraités, divorcés, veufs, le nombre de gens qui vivent seuls augmente.
The number of single, retired, divorced and widowed people who live alone is increasing.

Dans un sondage récent…
In a recent survey…

Beaucoup d'enfants voient leur père/mère refaire sa vie.
A lot of children see their father/mother starting a new relationship.

Beaucoup d'enfants habitent avec des demi-frères et des demi-sœurs.
A lot of children live with half-brothers and half-sisters.

Mes relations avec mes parents sont excellentes/bonnes/mauvaises.

I have an excellent/good/bad relationship with my parents.

> **KEY POINT**
>
> Note that **relations** in the sentence above means 'relationship'.

Si j'ai un problème, j'en parle avec mes amis, pas avec mes parents.

If I have a problem, I discuss it with friends, not with my parents.

À mon âge, les amis sont plus importants que la famille.

At my age, friends are more important than family.

À mon âge, on devrait pouvoir s'habiller comme on veut.

At my age, you should be able to dress as you want.

Elle est gâtée.

She is spoilt.

Avoir un frère plus âgé que vous, c'est embêtant.

It is annoying to have an older brother.

Je m'entends très bien avec mes parents.

I get on very well with my parents.

Je ne m'entends pas bien avec mon frère.

I do not get on with my brother.

> **KEY POINT**
>
> **S'entendre** means 'to get on with'.

Avec une famille nombreuse, on n'est jamais seul et ça me plaît.

In a large family, you are never alone and I like that.

Avec une famille nombreuse, on n'est jamais seul et ça ne me plaît pas parce qu'on n'a pas de vie privée et qu'il y a trop de bruit.

In a large family, you are never alone and I do not like it because you have no private life and there is too much noise.

Il y a des avantages et des désavantages.

There are advantages and disadvantages.

Si l'on est enfant unique, on se sent seul.

If you are an only child, you feel alone.

Mes parents ne veulent pas écouter mon point de vue.

My parents do not want to hear my point of view.

Si l'on a un problème, c'est la famille qui compte.

If you have a problem, it is good to have a family.

> **KEY POINT**
>
> **C'est la famille qui compte** literally means 'it is the family that counts'.

Je voudrais recevoir une somme fixe d'argent de poche.

I would like to get a set amount of pocket money.

Mes parents s'inquiètent trop.

My parents worry too much.

Mes parents veulent savoir avec qui je sors, où je vais et à quelle heure je rentre.

My parents want to know who I go out with, where I am going and what time I will get home.

Le sida, la drogue, l'alcool, le viol – il y a beaucoup de dangers pour les jeunes.

Aids, drugs, alcohol, rape – there are a lot of dangers facing young people.

Mes parents sont séparés et j'habite avec…

My parents are separated and I live with…

On prend rarement un repas ensemble.

We rarely eat together.

Les filles ont moins de liberté que les garçons.

Girls have less freedom than boys.

Mes parents ne s'occupent pas suffisamment de moi.

My parents do not look after me well.

Tout est/n'est pas rose dans ma famille.

Everything is/is not rosy in my family.

Il/elle est très sympathique/serviable/sévère/ennuyeux (-euse)/snob.

He/she is very nice/helpful/harsh/annoying/snobby.

Le parent idéal n'existe pas.

The ideal parent does not exist.

Il ne ment jamais.

He never lies.

> **KEY POINT**
>
> **Mentir** means 'to lie'.

Les apparences sont trompeuses.

Appearances are deceptive.

Je n'ai pas le droit de fréquenter les garçons.

I cannot go out with boys.

> **KEY POINT**
>
> Notice how the French say 'I cannot'. They say 'I haven't the right to'.

bruyant

Describing people (Descriptions des gens)

agressif (-ive) – aggressive	**calme** – quiet	**sensé(e)** – sensible
arrogant(e) – arrogant	**honnête** – honest	**timide** – shy
bavard(e) – talkative	**méchant(e)** – nasty	**triste** – sad
bruyant(e) – noisy	**poli(e)** – polite	

> **PROGRESS CHECK**
>
> Say or write the following in French:
> 1. In a recent survey
> 2. I have an excellent relationship with my parents.
> 3. She is spoilt.
> 4. There are advantages and disadvantages.
> 5. My parents worry too much.
>
> 1. Dans un sondage récent
> 2. Mes relations avec mes parents sont excellentes.
> 3. Elle est gâtée.
> 4. Il y a des avantages et des désavantages.
> 5. Mes parents s'inquiètent trop.

2.2 Future plans regarding marriage or partnership

LEARNING SUMMARY	**After studying this section, you should be able to:**
	• explain your plans or other people's plans for marriage or partnership
	• give views on marriage and parenthood

Marriage and partnership

AQA	✓
OCR	✓
EDEXCEL	✓
WJEC	✓
CCEA	✓

These sentences contain vocabulary and structures that will help you in the listening and reading exams, and in the controlled assessment.

Je vais décrire mon avenir.

I am going to describe my future.

Je ne me marierai pas avant 30 ans et j'aurai trois enfants.

I will not get married until I am 30 and I will have three children.

Je me marierai à l'âge de 24 ans.

I will get married at 24.

Je serai content(e) car je mènerai ma vie de la façon que j'ai choisie.

I will be happy because I will lead my life in the style I have chosen.

> **KEY POINT**
>
> Note that **mener ta vie** means 'to lead your life'.

J'habiterai une maison de luxe mais je ne serai pas marié(e).

I will have a luxury house but I will not get married.

Quand je quitterai l'école...[1]

When I leave school...

Quand j'aurai terminé mes études...[1]

When I have finished my studies...

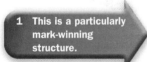

1 This is a particularly mark-winning structure.

> **KEY POINT**
>
> The French do not say 'when I leave' or 'when I have finished my studies'. They say 'when I will leave' or 'when I will have finished my studies'. So, remember you need to use the future tense with **quand** when future time is implied.

J'espère trouver un bon partenaire/une bonne partenaire.

I hope to find a nice partner.

Je serai marié(e) à une vedette.

I will marry a celebrity.

Plus tard je vais être heureux (-euse).

Later in life I am going to be happy.

Je serai homme/femme au foyer.

I will be a house husband/wife.

Mon/ma partenaire continuera de travailler pendant que je resterai à la maison.

My partner will carry on working while I stay at home.

Ce sera moi qui garderai les enfants à la maison.
It will be me who looks after the children at home.

> ### KEY POINT
>
> Note that in French you say 'it will be me who will keep' (first person singular).

Le mariage est important pour les rapports entre le couple.
Marriage is important for a couple's relationship.
Le mariage n'est pas important pour les rapports entre le couple.
Marriage is not important for a couple's relationship.
C'est un lien qui unit le couple.
It is a bond that unites the couple.

> ### KEY POINT
>
> **Unir** means 'to unite'.

Je vais me marier parce que c'est important pour les enfants d'avoir de la stabilité.
I am going to get married because stability is important for children.
Je ne comprends pas pourquoi on se marie.
I do not understand why people get married.
Il est plus simple de cohabiter sans se marier.
It is simpler to live together without getting married.
Je ne veux pas d'enfants.
I do not want children.
J'ai peur d'avoir des enfants.
I am frightened of having children.
Je veux bien me marier.
I am keen on getting married.
Je ne suis ni pour ni contre le mariage.
I am neither for nor against marriage.
Etre père/mère fait partie de mes projets.
I plan to be a parent.
Ce sera dans un an, dans cinq ans ou peut-être quand j'aurai soixante ans!
It will be in a year's time, in five years or perhaps when I am sixty!
Je veux des bébés, plein, plein, plein!
I want babies, loads of them!

> ### KEY POINT
>
> **Plein** really means 'full'. Used in the way shown above, it is an informal way of saying 'lots of'.

L'important, c'est l'amour.
The important thing is love.

> ### PROGRESS CHECK
>
> Say or write the following in French:
> 1. I want to get married.
> 2. I do not want to get married.
> 3. I want to live with a partner.
>
> 3. Je veux cohabiter.
> 2. Je ne veux pas me marier.
> 1. Je veux me marier.

2.3 Social issues

LEARNING SUMMARY

After studying this section, you should be able to:
- talk about homelessness, drugs, crime and smoking
- give views on social issues

Social issues

AQA	✓
OCR	✓
EDEXCEL	✗
WJEC	✓
CCEA	✓

You might like to do your speaking or writing controlled assessment on social issues. This topic might also appear in your listening and/or reading exam. You will find the following vocabulary and sentences invaluable.

Homelessness (L'absence de domicile)

démuni – deprived, destitute
un foyer d'hébergement – shelter for the homeless
l'immigré(e) – immigrant
le logement – housing

le préjugé – prejudice
priver – to deprive
les sans-abri (m, pl) – homeless people
le/la SDF (sans domicile fixe) – homeless person

> **KEY POINT**
>
> Literally, **sans-abri** means 'without shelter'.

En hiver, des lits sont réservés dans des foyers pour accueillir les sans-abri.
In winter, beds are kept in shelters to accommodate the homeless.
Mais au retour du printemps, ces lits ne sont plus disponibles.
But in spring, these beds are no longer available.
Certains foyers ferment, faute de moyens.
Some shelters close through lack of money.
Il a quitté le foyer familial pour venir s'installer dans une grande ville.
He left the family home to settle in a city.
Il gagne de l'argent en vendant *The Big Issue*.
He earns money by selling *The Big Issue*.

> **KEY POINT**
>
> **En** with the present participle means 'on doing' (something) or 'by doing' (something).

Il se trouve dans un cercle vicieux.
He is in a vicious circle.
Au Royaume-Uni, il y a cinq mille SDF.
In the UK, there are five thousand homeless people.

> **KEY POINT**
>
> The UK means England, Scotland, Wales and Northern Ireland.

Il se trouve sans amis et sans famille.

He has no friends or family.

Ce sont des personnes âgées, des jeunes, des immigrés et des mères avec leurs enfants.

They are old people, young people, immigrants and mothers with their children.

Ils vivent en plein air sans logement.

They live in the open without any accommodation.

Quelques-uns sont des malades mentaux.

Some are mentally ill.

le cambrioleur

Crime (La criminalité/Les infractions)

l'attentat (m) – attempt at crime

cambrioler – to burgle

le cambriolage – burglary

le cambrioleur – burglar

le malfaiteur – criminal

le vol – theft

le voleur – thief

J'ai vraiment peur de sortir de chez moi.

I am really frightened of going out.

KEY POINT

Avoir peur literally means 'to have fear'.

Dans les escaliers et à tous les coins de la rue...

On the stairways and on every corner of the street...

Il y a des bandes de voyous.

There are groups of thugs.

Ils vous regardent passer d'un air méchant.

They watch you go by menacingly.

La police devrait les arrêter.

The police should arrest them.

KEY POINT

Note that the conditional of **devoir** means 'should'.

J'ai vu un hold-up au centre-ville.

I saw a hold-up in town.

Quelqu'un a alerté la police.

Someone told the police.

Drugs (La drogue)

l'accro (m/f) – addict

le cannabis – cannabis

la cocaïne – cocaine

le comprimé – tablet

consommer – to take (drugs)

la désintoxication – detox

le/la drogué(e) – addict

la drogue douce – soft drug

la drogue dure – hard drug

se droguer – to take drugs

l'ecstasy (m) – ecstasy

l'héroïne (f) – heroin

la piqûre – injection

le/la toxicomane – addict

la toxicomanie – addiction

le/la trafiquant(e) – drug peddler

le comprimé

Dans ma ville, la drogue est un problème grave.
In my town, drugs are a huge problem.

> **KEY POINT**
>
> Note that in French they use the singular (**la drogue**) and we use the plural (drugs).

C'est la cause de beaucoup d'infractions.
It is the cause of a lot of crime.
Les toxicomanes doivent voler pour pouvoir acheter leur shoot.
The addicts have to steal to be able to buy their fix.
Les jeunes sont tentés parce que c'est interdit et ils croient que c'est cool de consommer de la drogue.
Young people are tempted because it is illegal and they think it is cool to take drugs.
Ils se droguent à cause de la pression des pairs.
They take drugs because of peer group pressure.
Les conséquences à long terme sont inconnues.
The long term consequences are unknown.

fumer

Smoking (Le tabagisme)

attirer les jeunes – attract young people
avoir un cancer – to get cancer
les fabricants de cigarettes – cigarette manufacturers

fumer – to smoke
interdire la publicité – to prohibit advertising
le tabagisme passif – passive smoking

Les derniers chiffres font peur.
The latest figures are alarming.

> **KEY POINT**
>
> Note that **faire peur** literally means 'to make fear'.

Maintenant, il y a plus de filles que de garçons qui fument.
Now, more girls than boys smoke.
On a interdit la publicité pour le tabac.
They have forbidden cigarette advertising.
Trois filles sur dix fument.
Three out of ten girls smoke.
Les fabricants de cigarettes essaient d'attirer les jeunes.
The cigarette manufacturers try to attract young people.
Les multinationales encouragent les jeunes à fumer.
The multinationals encourage youngsters to smoke.

> **KEY POINT**
>
> Notice that **encourager** takes **à** before the next infinitive.

Ils distribuent gratuitement les cigarettes.
They give out free cigarettes.
Les cigarettes me calment les nerfs.
Cigarettes calm my nerves.

Ils fument pour faire plus adulte.

They smoke to look grown up.

Je suis accro aux cigarettes.

I am hooked on cigarettes.

Le tabagisme passif m'inquiète.

Passive smoking worries me.

Il y a des gens qui fument pour faire comme leurs amis.

Some people smoke to be like their friends.

C'est dangereux pour les poumons.

It is dangerous for your lungs.

J'ai arrêté de fumer.

I stopped smoking.

> **KEY POINT**
>
> Note that **arrêter** takes **de** before the next infinitive.

C'est convivial.

It is sociable.

J'ai renoncé aux cigarettes, je ne fume plus.

I gave up cigarettes, I do not smoke anymore.

> **KEY POINT**
>
> 'To give up' is **renoncer** but you need **à** before the next word. In the sentence above, **à** and **les** have become **aux**.

Avant je fumais régulièrement.

I used to smoke regularly.

Ils ont arrêté les pubs pour le tabac à la télé.

They have stopped advertising cigarettes on TV.

C'est très mauvais pour la santé.

It is very bad for your health.

Good mark-winning 'avoir' structure.

Ils le font pour avoir l'air sophistiqué.

They smoke to look good.

> **KEY POINT**
>
> **Avoir l'air** means 'to look'. **Regarder** is the normal way of saying 'look', but when 'look' means 'appear' you must use **avoir l'air**.

Après avoir vu un film sur les dangers de fumer...

After seeing a film about the dangers of smoking...

> **KEY POINT**
>
> In the sentence above, you need to say 'after having seen...'

Je suis victime du tabagisme passif. Je suis devenu asthmatique.

I am a victim of passive smoking. I became asthmatic.

Le tabac contient des substances qui sont dangereuses pour le cœur, la peau et surtout les poumons.

Tobacco contains substances that are dangerous to the heart, the skin and especially the lungs.

Je n'ai pas envie de recommencer.

I do not want to start again.

Avoir envie really means 'to have desire to'. This is another useful **avoir** structure.

Personne n'a le droit de faire souffrir les autres.

Nobody has the right to make others suffer.

Ça pue.

It stinks.

Mes vêtements sentent mauvais.

My clothes smell bad.

Il a les dents et les doigts jaunes.

He has yellow teeth and fingers.

Il le trouve relaxant et cela combat le stress.

He finds it relaxing and it counteracts stress.

PROGRESS CHECK

Say or write the following in French:

1. Passive smoking
2. We have been burgled.
3. There are too many homeless people.
4. He has yellow teeth and fingers.
5. It is very bad for your health.

5. C'est très mauvais pour la santé.
4. Il a les dents et les doigts jaunes.
3. Il y a trop de gens sans abris.
2. On a été cambriolé.
1. Le tabagisme passif

2.4 Equality

LEARNING SUMMARY

After studying this section, you should be able to:

- talk about and give views on equality

Equality

AQA	✓
OCR	✗
EDEXCEL	✗
WJEC	✗
CCEA	✓

The following vocabulary and sentences will help you in the listening and reading exams, and in the controlled assessment.

Equality (L'égalité)

la condition féminine – the position of women

l'égalité des chances – equal opportunities

l'égalité des droits – equal rights

l'égalité des sexes – sexual equality

le fauteuil roulant – wheelchair

les handicapés – the disabled

Je trouve cela injuste.

I think that is unfair.

À travail égal, salaire égal.

Equal pay for equal work.

Les handicapés doivent avoir accès au bâtiment entier.

Disabled people must have access to the whole building.

Le gouvernement doit favoriser l'égalité des chances.

The government must promote equal opportunities.

Les femmes doivent rivaliser avec les hommes.

Women must compete with men.

Les hommes doivent traiter les femmes d'égal à égal.

Men must treat women as equals.

Il est chauvin.

He is a chauvinist.

Elle est féministe.

She is a feminist.

Les filles n'ont pas le droit de sortir alors que les garçons sortent tout le temps.

Girls cannot go out whilst boys go out all the time.

Les filles courent plus de dangers que les garçons.

Girls are at greater risk than boys.

PROGRESS CHECK

Say or write the following in French:

1. Equal opportunities
2. Chauvinist
3. As equals

3. D'égal à égal
2. Chauvin
1. L'égalité des chances

2.5 Grammar

LEARNING SUMMARY	After studying this section, you should be able to understand:
	• the present tense

The present tense

AQA	✓
OCR	✓
EDEXCEL	✓
WJEC	✓
CCEA	✓

Regular -er verbs

Learn the regular verbs first, as they are the easiest.

The endings are: **-e, -es, -e, -e, -ons, -ez, -ent, -ent**.

regarder	to look at, to watch
je regarde	I look at
tu regardes	you look at (informal singular)
il regarde	he looks at
elle regarde	she looks at
nous regardons	we look at
vous regardez	you look at (plural or polite singular)
ils regardent	they look at (masculine)
elles regardent	they look at (feminine)

The following verbs are like **regarder** (i.e. they are regular **-er** verbs).

arriver	to arrive	**trouver**	to find
manger	to eat	**marcher**	to walk
donner	to give	**préparer**	to prepare
chercher	to look for	**chanter**	to sing
habiter	to live	**commencer**	to begin

'Nous mangeons' = we eat: You have to add an '-e'.

Change 'je' to 'j'' before a vowel or 'h', e.g. 'j'arrive', 'j'habite'.

'Nous commençons' = we begin: You change 'c' to 'ç'.

PROGRESS CHECK

Say or write the following in French:

1. I live in London.
2. He walks slowly.
3. They (m) arrive late.
4. We sing well.
5. He prepares his books.
6. He gives money.
7. They (f) are watching TV.
8. We start at nine o'clock.
9. We are looking for a café.
10. We look for a café.

1. J'habite à Londres. 2. Il marche lentement. 3. Ils arrivent en retard.
4. Nous chantons bien. 5. Il prépare ses livres. 6. Il donne de l'argent.
7. Elles regardent la télé. 8. Nous commençons à neuf heures.
9. Nous cherchons un café. 10. Nous cherchons un café.

Regular -ir verbs

The endings for the present tense of regular **-ir** verbs are:

-is, -is, -it, -it, -issons, -issez, -issent, -issent.

finir

finir – to finish	
je finis	**nous finissons**
tu finis	**vous finissez**
il finit	**ils finissent**
elle finit	**elles finissent**

The following verbs are like **finir** (i.e. other regular **-ir** verbs).

bâtir	to build
choisir	to choose
remplir	to fill

PROGRESS CHECK

Say or write the following in French:

1. I am building a house.
2. You (singular) choose a book.
3. You (plural) fill the page.
4. She finishes her work.
5. We choose well.

1. Je bâtis une maison.
2. Tu choisis un livre.
3. Vous remplissez la page.
4. Elle finit son travail.
5. Nous choisissons bien.

vendre

Regular -re verbs

Regular **-re** verbs have the following endings: **-s, -s, –, –, -ons, -ez, -ent, -ent**.

vendre – to sell	
je vends	nous vendons
tu vends	vous vendez
il vend	ils vendent
elle vend	elles vendent

The following verbs are like **vendre** (i.e. regular **-re** verbs).

attendre	to wait for	perdre	to lose
entendre	to hear	répondre	to answer
rendre	to give back	descendre	to go down

PROGRESS CHECK

Say or write the following in French:
1. I wait for the bus.
2. You (singular) hear an explosion.
3. We give back the money.
4. They (m) lose the dog.
5. They (f) go down the road.
6. He replies to the invitation.
7. You (plural) sell the house.

1. J'attends le bus.
2. Tu entends une explosion.
3. Nous rendons l'argent.
4. Ils perdent le chien.
5. Elles descendent la rue.
6. Il répond à l'invitation.
7. Vous vendez la maison.

Irregular verbs

Most common verbs in French do not follow the above rules: they are irregular. You just have to learn them individually. Here are the essential ones.

boire

aller – to go	avoir – to have	boire – to drink
je vais	j'ai	je bois
tu vas	tu as	tu bois
il va	il a	il boit
elle va	elle a	elle boit
nous allons	nous avons	nous buvons
vous allez	vous avez	vous buvez
ils vont	ils ont	ils boivent
elles vont	elles ont	elles boivent
connaître – to know (a person/place)	croire – to believe	courir – to run
je connais	je crois	je cours
tu connais	tu crois	tu cours
il connaît	il croit	il court
elle connaît	elle croit	elle court
nous connaissons	nous croyons	nous courons
vous connaissez	vous croyez	vous courez
ils connaissent	ils croient	ils courent
elles connaissent	elles croient	elles courent

devoir – to have to, must	**dire** – to say, to tell	**dormir** – to sleep
je dois tu dois il doit elle doit nous devons vous devez ils doivent elles doivent	je dis tu dis il dit elle dit nous disons vous dites ils disent elles disent	je dors tu dors il dort elle dort nous dormons vous dormez ils dorment elles dorment
écrire – to write	**être** – to be	**faire** – to do, to make
j'écris tu écris il écrit elle écrit nous écrivons vous écrivez ils écrivent elles écrivent	je suis tu es il est elle est nous sommes vous êtes ils sont elles sont	je fais tu fais il fait elle fait nous faisons vous faites ils font elles font
lire – to read	**mettre** – to put	**pouvoir** – to be able
je lis tu lis il lit elle lit nous lisons vous lisez ils lisent elles lisent	je mets tu mets il met elle met nous mettons vous mettez ils mettent elles mettent	je peux tu peux il peut elle peut nous pouvons vous pouvez ils peuvent elles peuvent
partir – to leave	**prendre** – to take	**rire** – to laugh
je pars tu pars il part elle part nous partons vous partez ils partent elles partent	je prends tu prends il prend elle prend nous prenons vous prenez ils prennent elles prennent	je ris tu ris il rit elle rit nous rions vous riez ils rient elles rient
savoir – to know (a fact)	**recevoir** – to receive	**voir** – to see
je sais tu sais il sait elle sait nous savons vous savez ils savent elles savent	je reçois tu reçois il reçoit elle reçoit nous recevons vous recevez ils reçoivent elles reçoivent	je vois tu vois il voit elle voit nous voyons vous voyez ils voient elles voient

écrire

rire

vouloir

vouloir – to wish (a want)	**venir** – to come
je veux	**je viens**
tu veux	**tu viens**
il veut	**il vient**
elle veut	**elle vient**
nous voulons	**nous venons**
vous voulez	**vous venez**
ils veulent	**ils viennent**
elles veulent	**elles viennent**

PROGRESS CHECK

Say or write the following in French:

1. He is going into town.
2. We have a cat.
3. I drink a coffee.
4. They (m) know the teacher.
5. I believe you (singular) are right.
6. They (f) run in the garden.
7. You (singular) must pay.
8. You (plural) sleep in a bed.
9. We write many letters.
10. We are in the museum.
11. I am a student.
12. She reads a book.
13. I put the book on the table.
14. We can go to the cinema.
15. I leave at nine o'clock.
16. I take a shower.
17. We laugh because we are happy.
18. I know the time.
19. You (plural) receive many letters.
20. We see our friends.
21. You (singular) want to go to the cinema.
22. They (f) are coming at nine o'clock.

1. Il va en ville. 2. Nous avons un chat. 3. Je bois un café. 4. Ils connaissent le professeur. 5. Je crois que tu as raison. 6. Elles courent dans le jardin. 7. Tu dois payer. 8. Vous dormez dans un lit. 9. Nous écrivons beaucoup de lettres. 10. Nous sommes dans le musée. 11. Je suis étudiant(e). 12. Elle lit un livre. 13. Je mets le livre sur la table. 14. Nous pouvons aller au cinéma. 15. Je pars à neuf heures. 16. Je prends une douche. 17. Nous rions parce que nous sommes content(e)s. 18. Je sais l'heure. 19. Vous recevez beaucoup de lettres. 20. Nous voyons nos amis. 21. Tu veux aller au cinéma. 22. Elles viennent à neuf heures.

Venir de: to have just done something

The French do not say 'I have just done something'; they say 'I come from doing something', like this:

present tense of **venir** + **de** + the infinitive of the next verb

e.g.: I have just arrived = **je viens d'arriver**

PROGRESS CHECK

Say or write the following in French:
1. I have just seen the film.
2. He has just finished his work.
3. I have just finished my work.
4. They (m) have just bought the house.

1. Je viens de voir le film. 2. Il vient de terminer son travail. 3. Je viens de terminer mon travail. 4. Ils viennent d'acheter la maison.

Sample controlled assessment

Speaking

1 Track 7 You are going to have a conversation with your teacher about smoking. Your teacher will ask you to discuss…

- your opinion
- the government's contribution
- why so many youngsters smoke
- how you feel about passive smoking.

Teacher: Tu fumes?

Student: Absolument pas.[16] C'est si[18] mauvais pour la santé. Avant, je fumais[13] régulièrement. J'étais accro aux cigarettes, mais après avoir vu[8] un film sur les dangers du tabac, j'ai arrêté de fumer. J'ai tout à fait[16] renoncé aux cigarettes, et je ne fume plus.[24] Je ne fume plus depuis[26] deux ans.

Teacher: Pourquoi?

Student: Le tabac contient des substances qui[30] sont dangereuses pour le cœur, la peau et surtout les poumons, donc je n'ai pas envie de[1] recommencer. Les derniers chiffres font peur. Maintenant, il y a plus de filles que de garçons qui fument. Trois filles sur dix fument. Malgré[19] les conseils de mes parents, ma sœur fume et ça pue. Ses vêtements sentent mauvais et elle a les dents et les doigts jaunes. C'est si[18] dégoûtant. Mais elle dit qu'elle est sur le point d'arrêter.[21]

Teacher: Et le gouvernement?

Student: On a interdit la publicité pour le tabac. Ils ont arrêté les pubs pour le tabac à la télé. Les fabricants de cigarettes essaient d'attirer les jeunes. Même[16] les multinationales encouragent les jeunes à fumer. En Afrique, ils distribuent gratuitement les cigarettes. Quel scandale! Quel cauchemar![9] Malheureusement,[16] les fabricants de tabac financent la Formule 1, et les jeunes peuvent voir des publicités de cigarettes à la télé. Il faut que le gouvernement fasse[25] plus pour aider et protéger les jeunes. Il devrait[14] augmenter le prix des cigarettes.

Teacher: Pourquoi est-ce que tant de jeunes fument?

Student: Ils fument pour faire[31] plus adulte. Il y a des gens qui fument pour faire comme leurs amis. Ils le[32] font pour avoir l'air sophistiqué. Ils aiment fumer quand ils sont avec leurs amis. Ils disent que les cigarettes leur calment les nerfs. Ils trouvent cela relaxant, et cela combat le stress. S'il y a un problème, sans perdre de temps,[5] ils sortent les cigarettes.

Teacher: Et le tabagisme passif?

Student: En voyant[7] les gens qui fument, je me fâche. Le tabagisme passif m'inquiète. Je suis victime du tabagisme passif, je suis devenu asthmatique. Personne n'a le droit[24] de faire souffrir les autres.

Teacher: Tu as un conseil à donner aux enfants?

Student: Oui. Avant de commencer[6] à fumer, réfléchissez! C'est la pire chose[23] qu'on puisse faire. Si vous fumez, vous allez le regretter.[12]

Turn to page 155 for a translation of this passage.

Turn to page 155 for a translation of this passage.

Examiner's comments

This student has produced an A* piece of work by including the following points from the '32 points for improving your grade' on pages 8–10:

1 An 'avoir' structure

5 'Sans' + the infinitive

6 'Avant de'

7 'En' + the present participle

8 'Après avoir' + the past participle

9 An exclamation

12 The future tense

13 Good use of the imperfect tense

14 Use of a conditional

16 Four examples of impressive vocabulary being used, e.g. 'absolument pas' instead of 'non'. Watch the spelling of 'malheureusement' – there are two letter 'u's in it.

18 The use of 'si' instead of 'très'

19 'Malgré'

21 'Sur le point de'

23 A superlative

24 Two good uses of negatives

25 An excellent example of the subjunctive

26 A 'depuis' structure

30 A connecting word

31 'Pour' + the infinitive

32 Good use of a pronoun

Sample controlled assessment

Writing

1 Write about your future plans regarding marriage or partnership. You could write about...

- your opinions on how to be happy
- your plans for marriage or otherwise
- the ideal partner
- how work will affect your relationship
- your views on cohabitation.

Je vais décrire[12] mon avenir. Je vais être vraiment[18] heureux (-euse)! Ce sera dans un an, dans cinq ans ou peut-être quand j'aurai[12] soixante ans, mais c'est le bonheur que je cherche. Je serai content(e) car[30] je mènerai[12] ma vie de la façon que j'ai choisie.[16] Je voudrais me marier.

Je ne me marierai pas avant 30 ans et j'aurai au moins[16] trois enfants. Être père/mère fait partie de mes projets bien que j'aie peur[25] d'avoir des enfants. Je veux des bébés, plein, plein, plein, mais avant de[6] me marier j'ai envie de[1] voyager partout dans le monde.[16]

Après avoir vu[8] le monde, l'important, c'est[16] l'amour. J'habiterai une maison de luxe parce que quand je quitterai l'école, j'espère trouver un bon partenaire/une bonne partenaire. En le/la[32] trouvant,[7] je saurai[12] tout de suite si c'est la personne pour moi. Quand j'aurai terminé mes études, je me marierai peut-être à une vedette. Je serai homme/femme au foyer. Mon/ma partenaire continuera de travailler pendant que[30] je resterai à la maison. C'est moi qui garderai les enfants à la maison.

Pour moi, le mariage est important pour les rapports entre le couple. C'est un lien qui unit le couple. Je vais me marier parce que c'est important pour les enfants d'avoir de la stabilité.[3] Pour un enfant, la stabilité est la chose la plus importante.[23] Je viens de[20] discuter ce sujet avec ma sœur. Ma sœur dit qu'elle ne comprend pas pourquoi on se marie. Quelle horreur![9] Elle dit qu'il est plus simple[22] de cohabiter sans se marier.[5] Elle est sur le point d'aller[21] cohabiter avec son petit ami. Je ne cohabiterai jamais[24] malgré le fait que[19] mes parents avaient cohabité[17] avant de se marier. Ils cohabitaient[13] depuis[26] cinq ans. Mon frère n'est ni pour ni contre[24] le mariage et il ne veut pas d'enfants malheureusement.[16]

Turn to page 155 for a translation of this passage.

Turn to page 155 for a translation of this passage.

Examiner's comments

This model example implements many of the '32 points for improving your grade' on pages 8–10:

1. An 'avoir' structure
3. One of many points of view and justifications in this piece of work
5. 'Sans' + the infinitive
6. An 'avant de' structure
7. 'En' + present participle
8. 'Après avoir' + the past participle
9. An exclamation
12. A good variety of future tense structures
13. An example of the imperfect
16. Impressive vocabulary and structures, e.g. 'au moins', 'partout dans le monde', 'l'important, c'est', 'malheureusement'
17. An example of a pluperfect
18. 'Vraiment' here is much better than 'très'
19. A 'malgré' structure
20. 'Venir de'
21. A 'sur le point de' structure
22. A comparative has been used
23. An example of a superlative
24. Good examples of negatives
25. Extra marks for a subjunctive
26. 'Depuis'
30. Good connectives used here
32. Good use of a pronoun

Exam practice questions

Listening

1 🔘 Track 8   Karine is talking about her family. Answer the questions by filling in the gaps **in English**. There are **two** sections.

Section 1

(a)   Her little brother is ……………………………………… years old.   **(1)**

(b)   She gets annoyed with him because he ……………………………………… and is always in

………………………………… .   **(2)**

(c)   He had a ……………………………………… for his birthday.   **(1)**

Section 2

(d)   Her parents accept that she is ……………………………………… .   **(1)**

(e)   She is allowed to ……………………………… and to ……………………………… .   **(2)**

(f)   Next year she plans to ……………………………………………………………… .   **(1)**

WJEC Foundation Tier

2 🔘 Track 9   Listen to this interview with Audrey Tautou, the actress, star of the films *Amélie* and *The Da Vinci Code*. Answer the questions **in English**. **There are three sections.**

Section 1

(a)   What was Audrey's childhood like?

……

(b)   What is her attitude towards her family?

……

Section 2

(c)   What did her parents buy her as a present after her exams?

……

(d)   Why did she arrive late for the casting of *Vénus Beauté*?

……

Section 3

(e)   In what way does she think she's like Amélie?

……

(f)   What does she think about being famous?

………   **(6)**

WJEC Higher Tier

Exam practice questions

3 **Track 10** Listen to the three people giving their views about society. Answer the following questions, ticking the correct boxes where required.

(a) M. Laudic is...

   A lazy ☐

   B difficult ☐

   C optimistic ☐

(b) What does M. Laudic think of the interviewer?

....

(c) What does M. Laudic think of the idea of giving money to the unemployed?

....

(d) What does he think of the unemployed?

....

(e) Mme. Bernard is...

   A lazy ☐

   B difficult ☐

   C optimistic ☐

(f) What does Mme. Bernard think has improved in the town?

....

(g) How does Mme. Bernard think people have changed?

....

(h) How does she see the future?

....

(i) M. Renault is...

   A pessimistic ☐

   B difficult ☐

   C optimistic ☐

(j) When he sees the world what does he want to do?

.... **(10)**

Exam practice questions

Reading

1 Read the magazine article below about young people and how easy it is to get permission to go out, then answer the questions that follow.

Quelques jeunes apportent leur opinion sur leurs relations avec leurs parents. En voici quelques extraits.

Je veux sortir!

Je ne peux rien faire. Partir en week-end, aller à une soirée, passer voir une copine. Je dois en parler avec mes parents au moins trois jours avant et souvent je me retrouve face à un refus de leur part au dernier moment. **Anne, 16 ans**

Mes parents ne comprennent pas le fait que je veuille sortir. Pour moi, les copains sont ma raison de vivre. Mes parents disent que je dois mériter chaque sortie, c'est comme une récompense. Il est fatigant de se disputer tout le temps. **Pierre, 15 ans**

Je n'ai pas de problèmes avec mes parents à propos des sorties. Je sors comme je veux le week-end, mais pendant la semaine je fais mes devoirs. Ils me demandent simplement de les prévenir quand je pense rentrer après minuit et puis aussi de ne pas rentrer dans un état d'ivresse et d'assurer le lendemain (le dimanche), de ne pas dormir toute la journée. **Edgar, 17 ans**

J'ai un accord avec mes parents. Je peux sortir 2 week-ends par mois. Concert, boîte de nuit ou fête chez des copains… Il faut que je précise l'heure de mon retour. Moi je paie mes sorties avec mon argent de poche. J'apprends à faire des choix. **Céline, 16 ans**

(a) **(i)** What must Anne do if she wants to go out?

....

(ii) What might happen at the last moment?

.... **(2)**

(b) What is Pierre's reason for living? .... **(1)**

(c) What must Pierre do if he wants to go out? .... **(1)**

(d) What does Pierre find tiring? .... **(1)**

(e) When does Edgar go out? .... **(1)**

(f) Before Edgar goes out, what must he do?

.... **(1)**

(g) When Edgar gets home, what is expected of him? .... **(1)**

(h) What must Edgar not do on Sundays? .... **(1)**

(i) What bargain has Céline struck with her parents? .... **(1)**

(j) Name the three places Céline likes to go.

(i) .... **(ii)** .... **(iii)** .... **(3)**

(k) What must Céline do before she goes out? .... **(1)**

(l) Who pays for Céline's nights out? .... **(1)**

(m) What has Céline learned to do? .... **(1)**

Exam practice questions

2 Sophie has written to *Miss Star* magazine about her best friend in school. There are five gaps for you to fill in from the words in the box below. **Write the correct word** next to the letter in the answer spaces below.

Chers Lecteurs de Miss Star!

Salut! Je m´(x) Sophie. Je vais vous parler de ma meilleure copine Natalie.

Natalie est de (a) moyenne avec les yeux bleus et les cheveux (b). Au collège elle est dans la même classe que moi et nous (c) toutes les deux les maths et le dessin.

Elle aime observer les (d) dans le jardin. Comme moi elle aime regarder surtout les feuilletons et les émissions de musique.

Le père de Sophie ne travaille pas, donc il est au (e) mais sa mère est informaticienne dans un bureau à Brive.

J´aime beaucoup mon amie Natalie!

Write your answers here:

Example: (x) *appelle*

(a) ....

(b) ....

(c) ....

(d) ....

(e) .... **(5)**

Choose your answers from this box:

ceinture	aimons	gros	crions	taille	oiseaux	blonds
station-service	chômage	arrête	appelle	Pays de Galles		

WJEC Foundation Tier

Exam practice questions

3 Read this letter from Asim and **answer the questions**.

> J'habite dans le Midi depuis sept ans et autrefois j'habitais au Maroc. Je vais à un collège mixte et je dois dire que les évènements du 11 septembre n'ont pas beaucoup touché ma vie. Nous sommes une cinquantaine de Marocains dans mon collège et nous nous entendons bien avec tous les Français. Nous discutons les grandes questions du jour et nous nous montrons un grand respect. Mes amis comprennent que nous pratiquons une autre religion qu'eux (s'ils la pratiquent du tout) et il y en a qui ont commencé à apprendre ma langue, l'arabe, la langue de ma famille. Le seul problème, c'est quand nous voulons aller au Maroc en avion on doit arriver très tôt à l'aéroport à cause des contrôles de sécurité. La première chose que je fais quand j'atterris au Maroc, c'est de téléphoner à ma petite amie parce qu'elle me manque.

(a) How long has Asim been living in France?

A Seven months ☐ **B** Seven years ☐ **C** All his life ☐

(b) How many Moroccans are in his school?

A 500 ☐ **B** 5 ☐ **C** 50 ☐

(c) What does he talk about with his friends?

A The weather ☐ **B** Current affairs ☐ **C** Respect ☐

(d) What language does he speak at home?

A Arabic ☐ **B** French ☐ **C** Moroccan ☐

(e) How does he travel to Morocco?

A Boat ☐ **B** Hovercraft ☐ **C** Plane ☐

(f) What does he have to do because of the security checks?

A Travel with his parents ☐

B Arrive early for departure ☐

C Always carry his passport ☐

(g) What does he do as soon as he arrives in Morocco?

A Phones his grandmother ☐

B Phones his girlfriend ☐

C Recharges his phone ☐

(7)

WJEC Higher Tier

3 Leisure, free time and the media

The following topics are covered in this chapter:

- Free time activities
- Shopping, money, fashion and trends
- Advantages and disadvantages of new technology
- Grammar

3.1 Free time activities

LEARNING SUMMARY

After studying this section, you should be able to:

- talk about your interest in sport and your hobbies
- give reasons why you like or dislike various sports
- talk about your favourite films and TV programmes
- talk about music and whether you play musical instruments

Sport and leisure

AQA	✓
OCR	✓
EDEXCEL	✓
WJEC	✓
CCEA	✓

Sport and leisure is a favourite topic of examiners. It is likely that you will be asked about your sporting interests in the controlled speaking and writing assessments. You should make sure that you can talk about your favourite sports, and be able to say which sports you like and which you dislike. You must be able to say how you spend your free time, how you spent your free time (for example, last weekend) and how you will spend your free time (for example, next weekend). You will also find the following vocabulary invaluable for the listening and reading exams.

le basket

Sports (Les sports)

l'alpinisme (m) – climbing
l'athlétisme (m) – athletics
le basket – basketball
le cyclisme – cycling
l'équitation (f) – horse-riding
faire du cheval – to go riding
le football – football
le handball – handball
le hockey – hockey
la natation – swimming

la pêche – fishing
la planche à roulettes – skateboarding
la planche à voile – windsurfing
le rugby – rugby
le ski nautique – water-skiing
les sports d'hiver – winter sports
le tennis – tennis
la voile – sailing
le volley – volleyball

Sports words

le ballon – ball
le champion – champion
le concours – competition
le/la cycliste – cyclist

l'équipe (f) – team
le/la joueur (-euse) – player
le match – match
le spectateur – spectator

le cycliste

gagner

nager

Sports verbs

aimer bien – to quite like
assister – to be present at
attraper – to catch
courir – to run
gagner – to win

grimper – to climb
s'intéresser à – to be interested in
jouer au football – to play football

nager – to swim
patiner – to skate
pêcher – to fish
perdre – to lose
sauter – to jump

la chanteuse

le jardinage

le patin à roulettes

Leisure (Les loisirs)

avec plaisir – with pleasure
le bal – dance
la boîte de nuit – night club
les boules (f, pl) – bowls
la boum – party
le café – café
la canne à pêche – fishing rod
la cassette – cassette
le centre de loisirs – leisure centre
le centre sportif – sports centre
la chanson – song
le/la chanteur (-euse) – singer
le cinéma – cinema
le cirque – circus
le club – club
le concert – concert
les échecs (m, pl) – chess
la fête – party
la galerie de jeux – amusement arcade
le jardin zoologique – zoo

le jardinage – gardening
le jeu – game
le jeu électronique – computer game
le jeu-vidéo – video game
le jouet – toy
la location (de vélos) – (bike) hire
louer – to hire
la maison des jeunes – youth club
le passe-temps – hobby
le patin (à roulettes) – (roller) skate
la planche à voile – surfboard
la promenade – walk
le sac à dos – rucksack
le maillot de bain – swimming costume
le stade – stadium
le vélo – bicycle
le VTT (vélo tout terrain) – mountain bike
le week-end – weekend

Leisure verbs

s'amuser – to have a good time
se baigner – to bathe
bavarder – to chat
bricoler – to do DIY
bronzer – to sunbathe
chanter – to sing
écouter – to listen
faire des promenades – to go for walks

faire du lèche-vitrines – to go
   window shopping
faire le jardinage – to do
   the gardening
faire une promenade – to go for a walk
jouer aux cartes – to play cards
jouer de la musique – to play music
sortir – to go out

PROGRESS CHECK

Say or write the following in French:

1. I play football on Saturdays.
2. I prefer tennis.
3. I like going for walks.
4. I hate gardening.
5. I never play tennis.
6. I go out on Saturday evenings.

1. Je joue au football le samedi. 2. Je préfère le tennis. 3. J'aime faire des promenades. 4. Je déteste le jardinage. 5. Je ne joue jamais au tennis. 6. Je sors le samedi soir.

Conversation

AQA	✓
OCR	✓
EDEXCEL	✓
WJEC	✓
CCEA	✓

The following are commonly-asked questions in the controlled speaking assessment. Practise these sentences with a friend.

Quel est ton passe-temps favori?
J'aime jouer au tennis.[1]
Où est-ce que tu joues au tennis?
Je joue dans le parc.
Tu joues avec qui?
Je joue avec mes amis.
Tu vas souvent au cinéma?
J'y vais quand j'ai de l'argent.
Tu aimes le jardinage?
Je déteste le jardinage.
Quel sport préfères-tu?
Je préfère le hockey.

1. You should add a few more hobbies, e.g. 'et regarder la télé'.

Conversation

AQA	✓
OCR	✓
EDEXCEL	✓
WJEC	✓
CCEA	✓

KEY POINT

Use a variety of tenses and give opinions.

Décris tes passe-temps.
J'ai beaucoup de passe-temps. J'aime jouer au football/hockey/tennis/ basket. J'aime aussi regarder la télé, lire, aller au cinéma et sortir avec mes amis.
Quel est ton sport favori?
Mon sport favori est la natation. Normalement, je vais à la piscine le samedi avec mes amis.

1 This is your chance to use as many present tenses as you can.

2 This is your chance to use as many perfect tenses (see pages 92–93) as you can.

3 This is your chance to use as many future tenses (see page 120) as you can.

Qu'est-ce que tu lis?

Je lis des romans mais aussi des magazines et des journaux.

Qu'est-ce que tu fais le soir après tes devoirs?[1]

Je lis, je regarde la télé, j'écoute de la musique, je fais une promenade et je vais voir mon ami.

Qu'est-ce que tu as fait hier soir après tes devoirs?[2]

J'ai lu, j'ai regardé la télé, j'ai écouté de la musique, j'ai fait une promenade et je suis allé(e) voir mon ami.

Qu'est-ce que tu vas faire ce soir après tes devoirs?[3]

Je lirai, je regarderai la télé, j'écouterai de la musique, je ferai une promenade et j'irai voir mon ami.

PROGRESS CHECK

Say or write the following in French:

1 I like tennis and going out.

2 Yesterday I went out with my friends.

3 I will go out with my friends on Saturday.

1. J'aime le tennis et j'aime sortir. 2. Hier je suis sorti(e) avec mes amis. 3. Samedi je sortirai avec mes amis.

Cinema and TV

AQA ✓
OCR ✓
EDEXCEL ✓
WJEC ✓
CCEA ✓

Film and TV is a likely topic for your controlled speaking and writing assessments. You will probably be asked about your favourite type of film or TV programme. In the reading exam, you might be given a TV schedule or a film schedule and asked questions about which programmes are shown at which times.

Cinema and TV (Le cinéma et la TV)

le film d'amour

l'acteur (m) – actor
l'actrice (f) – actress
les actualités (f, pl) – news
la chaîne – TV channel
la comédie – comedy
le dessin animé – cartoon
l'écran (m) – screen
l'émission (f) – programme
le feuilleton – soap, TV series
le film comique – comedy film
le film d'amour – romantic film
le film d'aventures – adventure film
le film d'épouvante – horror film

le film d'horreur – horror film
le film policier – detective film
les informations (f, pl) – news
les publicités (f, pl) – adverts
la séance – performance
sous-titré – sub-titled
la télé par satellite – satellite TV
le théâtre – theatre
la vedette – star
en version française – dubbed in French
en version originale – not dubbed
le western – western

Conversation

AQA ✓
OCR ✓
EDEXCEL ✓
WJEC ✓
CCEA ✓

1 This is your chance to give an opinion and to justify it.

Quelle sorte de films aimes-tu?[1]

J'aime les films d'aventure. Je n'aime pas les films d'amour parce qu'ils sont trop sentimentaux. Les films d'épouvante et les films de guerre sont trop barbants.

Music and musical instruments

AQA	✓
OCR	✓
EDEXCEL	✓
WJEC	✓
CCEA	✓

If your teacher knows that you like music or that you play an instrument, you may well be asked about music in your controlled speaking assessment. You need to be able to express your likes, dislikes and preferences. You might like to use a famous musician as the subject of your presentation, if you are doing one, or for your controlled writing assessment. Music may also appear in the listening and reading exams.

Musical terms

le disc compact – compact disc
la disco(thèque) – disco
la hi-fi – hi-fi
jouer du piano – to play the piano

le/la musicien(ne) – musician
la musique classique – classical music
l'orchestre (m) – orchestra
pop – pop

la guitare   le piano   le violon

Musical instruments (Les instruments de musique)

la batterie – drums
le clavier – keyboard
la flûte à bec – recorder
la guitare – guitar

le piano – piano
la trompette – trumpet
le violon – violin

Conversation

AQA	✓
OCR	✓
EDEXCEL	✓
WJEC	✓
CCEA	✓

🎵 **Tu sais jouer d'un instrument de musique?**
🎵 Je sais jouer de la guitare.
🎵 **Quelle sorte de musique préfères-tu?**
🎵 Je préfère la musique pop.

3.2 Shopping, money, fashion and trends

LEARNING SUMMARY	**After studying this section, you should be able to:** • talk about shops and shopping • talk about the post office, bank and money • describe clothes, fashion and trends

Shops and shopping

AQA	✓
OCR	✓
EDEXCEL	✓
WJEC	✓
CCEA	✓

You will find the following vocabulary particularly useful for answering questions in the listening and reading exams.

le marchand de fruits et légumes

Shops (Les magasins)

l'agence de voyages (f) – travel agent's
l'alimentation (f) – grocer's
le boucher/la bouchère – butcher
la boucherie – butcher's
le boulanger/la boulangère – baker
la boulangerie – baker's
la boutique – shop
le bureau de poste – post office
le bureau de tabac – tobacconist's
la charcuterie – pork butcher's
la confiserie – sweet shop
la crêperie – pancake stall
l'épicerie (f) – grocer's
l'épicier (m)/l'épicière (f) – grocer

le grand magasin – department store
l'hypermarché (m) – hypermarket, superstore
la librairie – bookshop
le magasin – shop
le marchand de fruits et légumes – greengrocer
le marché – market
la papeterie – stationer's
la parfumerie – perfume shop
la pâtisserie – cake shop
la pharmacie – chemist's
le pharmacien – chemist
la poissonnerie – fishmonger's
le supermarché – supermarket

Shopping (Le shopping)

le parfum

l'achat (m) – purchase
Avec ça? – Anything else?
C'est combien? – How much is it?
C'est tout – That's all
le/la client(e) – customer
l'étage (m) – floor, storey
faire les commissions/courses – to do the shopping
fermé(e) – closed
gratuit(e) – free
le morceau – piece
ouvert(e) – open

le panier – basket
le parfum – perfume
pas très cher – not very expensive
pas trop cher – not too expensive
le prix – price
la promotion – special offer
le rayon – shop department
le sac – bag
les soldes (f, pl) – sales
au sous-sol – in the basement/cellar
la taille – size
la tranche – slice

Conversation

AQA	✓
OCR	✓
EDEXCEL	✓
WJEC	✓
CCEA	✓

🔵 **Tu aimes faire du shopping?**
🔵 J'aime bien ça si j'ai de l'argent.
🔵 **Tu aimes faire les commissions?**
🔵 Je n'aime pas aller aux magasins mais j'aime aller au supermarché.

The post office

AQA	✓
OCR	✓
EDEXCEL	✓
WJEC	✓
CCEA	✓

At the post office (À la poste)

la boîte aux lettres – post box
la carte postale – postcard
le courrier – mail
le facteur – postman

le paquet – packet, parcel
le timbre (d'un euro) – (one-euro) stamp

Banks and money

AQA	✓
OCR	✓
EDEXCEL	✓
WJEC	✓
CCEA	✓

At the bank (À la banque)

l'argent (m) – money
un billet de dix-euros – a 10-euro note
le bureau de change – foreign exchange office
la caisse – cashpoint, till
la carte bancaire – banker's card
la carte de crédit – credit card

le chèque de voyage – traveller's cheque
la commission – commission
la livre sterling – pound sterling
la monnaie – change, currency
la pièce – coin
la pièce d'identité – ID

remplir une fiche

Bank verbs

accepter – to accept
changer – to change

remplir une fiche – to fill in a form
signer – to sign

Conversation

AQA	✓
OCR	✓
EDEXCEL	✓
WJEC	✓
CCEA	✓

🎧 **Tu fais des économies?**

🎧 Toutes les semaines je mets £10 à la banque. Je fais des économies pour acheter un ordinateur, un baladeur MP3 et pour partir en vacances.

🎧 **Et comment tu dépenses le reste?**

🎧 Je me paie des sorties: j'achète des CD, du maquillage, des vêtements et je prends des leçons de conduite. De temps en temps je donne de l'argent aux œuvres caritatives pour aider les animaux.

> **KEY POINT**
>
> **Je me paie** means 'I pay for myself' or 'I treat myself to'.

Fashion and trends

AQA ✓
OCR ✓
EDEXCEL ✓
WJEC ✓
CCEA ✓

The following vocabulary and sentences will help you in the listening and reading exams, and in the controlled assessment.

Clothes and accessories (Les vêtements et les accessoires)

le collier

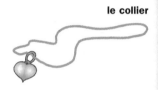

la montre

les baskets (f, pl) – trainers
le blouson – jacket
la boucle d'oreille – earring
la casquette – cap
la ceinture – belt
le chapeau – hat
les chaussettes (f, pl) – socks
les chaussures (f, pl) – shoes
la chemise – shirt
le chemisier – blouse
le collant – tights
le collier – necklace
le costume – suit
la cravate – tie
la culotte – knickers
l'écharpe (f) – (neck) scarf
le foulard – (head) scarf
l'imperméable (m) – raincoat
le jean – jeans

la jupe – skirt
le jogging – tracksuit
le maillot de bain – bathing suit
le manteau – coat
le maquillage – make-up
la montre – watch
le pantalon – trousers
le pull – jumper
la robe – dress
le rouge à lèvres – lipstick
le ruban – ribbon
le sac à main – handbag
le slip – briefs
le short – shorts
le soutien-gorge – bra
le sweat-shirt – sweatshirt
le T-shirt – T-shirt
la veste – jacket

Materials (Les matières)

en coton – (made of) cotton
en cuir – (made of) leather
en soie – (made of) silk
en laine – (made of) wool

en jean – (made of) denim
en polyester – (made of) polyester
en velours – (made of) velvet

Style (Le style)

à carreaux – checked
court(e) – short
écossais(e) – tartan
étroit(e) – tight
large – baggy

long(ue) – long
le look gothique –
   goth look
le look rappeur –
   rapper look

à pois – with spots,
   spotted
à rayures – with stripes,
   stripy
uni(e) – plain

Out shopping

Ce pantalon en cuir ne te va pas.
These leather trousers do not suit you.
Je cherche une chemise en soie.
I am looking for a silk shirt.
Vous faites quelle taille?
What size are you?
Je cherche des baskets.
I am looking for trainers.
Vous faites quelle pointure?
What size (shoes) are you?
Je peux l'essayer/les essayer?
Can I try it/them on?
Où est la cabine d'essayage?
Where are the changing rooms?
Avez-vous la même chose en rouge?
Have you got the same thing in red?
Je regrette, il n'y en a plus.
I am sorry, we haven't got any more.

Other useful sentences

Il porte des vêtements sombres et des bottes noires.
He wears dark clothes and black boots.
Il porte un T-shirt large et un pantalon trop long avec des baskets bleues.
He wears a baggy T-shirt and trousers that are too long with blue trainers.
Pour aller au bureau, elle va acheter...
To go to the office, she is going to buy...
Pour assister au mariage de sa soeur, elle va mettre...
To attend her sister's wedding, she is going to wear...

> **KEY POINT**
>
> **Assister** means 'to assist', but it also means 'to attend'.

Je mets mon nouveau blouson.
I am putting on my new jacket.
Elle met un pantalon parce qu'elle n'aime pas porter des jupes.
She is putting on trousers because she does not like wearing skirts.

Conversation

AQA	✓
OCR	✓
EDEXCEL	✓
WJEC	✓
CCEA	✓

🗨 **Tu aimes être à la mode?**

🗨 J'adore être à la mode mais ça coûte si cher.

🗨 **Tu paierais plus cher un vêtement parce que sa marque est connue?**

🗨 Oui, c'est normal. Il faut que je sois dans le coup.

🗨 **Tu préfères la marque écrite devant, dans le dos ou sur l'étiquette?**

🗨 Dans le dos.

🗨 **En gros, en petit ou en minuscule?**

🗨 En gros.

🗨 **Tu préfères le look rappeur, le gothique ou quoi?**

🗨 Les deux looks m'intriguent mais je préfère mon look à moi.

🗨 **Tu recherches les étiquettes 'fabriqué en Europe' ou tu achètes des habits fabriqués par des ouvriers africains payés huit euros par jour?**

🗨 Je n'achète que Nike et Adidas.

> **KEY POINT**
>
> **Marque** means 'make'.
> **Il faut que je sois dans le coup** means 'I have to be up to date'.
> **Étiquette** means 'label'.
> Note that **ne … que** means 'only', so **je n'achète que** means 'I only buy'.

3.3 Advantages and disadvantages of new technology

LEARNING SUMMARY	**After studying this section, you should be able to:** • talk about computers, mobile phones and other gadgets • explain the advantages of new technology • explain the disadvantages of new technology

New technology

AQA	✓
OCR	✓
EDEXCEL	✓
WJEC	✓
CCEA	✓

The following vocabulary and sentences will help you in the listening and reading exams, and in the controlled assessment.

ICT (L'informatique)

le téléphone portable

l'adresse (f) – address

l'appareil photo numérique (m) –
   digital camera

le blog – blog

la carte mémoire – SIM card

la cartouche – ink cartridge

le clavier – keyboard

la clé USB – USB memory stick

cliquer – to click

le disque – compact CD

l'écran tactile (m) – touch screen

l'e-mail (m), le courrier électronique
   – e-mail

équipé de... – equipped with...

la facture – bill

le forum – newsgroup

le GPS – sat-nav

gratuit(e) – free

l'imprimante (f) – printer

Internet haut débit – broadband

le lecteur de DVD – DVD player

le lecteur MP3, baladeur MP3 –
   MP3 player

le lien – link

le logiciel – software

la mémoire – memory

l'ordinateur (m) – computer,
   portable laptop

la pile – battery

le serveur – server

le site – website

la sonnerie – ring tone

la souris – mouse

télécharger – to download

le téléphone avec forfait – (phone)
   contract

le téléphone portable – mobile phone

le téléphone prépayé – pre-paid (phone)

le texto, le minimessage – text

la toile – the Web

The advantages of new technology – what people say

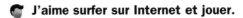

🖱 Internet à l'école – c'est génial, parce que ça nous permet de faire des recherches pour un devoir.

🖱 Nous avons notre propre site à l'école.

🖱 C'est un excellent moyen de communiquer avec tout le monde.

> **KEY POINT**
>
> **Moyen** means 'way'.

🖱 J'aime surfer sur Internet et jouer.

🖱 L'Internet est utile pour contacter des jeunes dans le monde entier.

🖱 Ça nous aide à trouver des correspondants et ça permet de pratiquer une autre langue.

🖱 Nous allons bientôt créer notre propre site.

🖱 Il est intéressant de naviguer sur le Net.

🖱 C'est pratique, cela ne fait pas de bruit.

🖱 Les parents sont rassurés, ils peuvent se mettre en contac s'ils veulent.

🖱 Avec mon nouveau portable, je peux surfer sur Internet.

🖱 Le téléphone portable est très utile pour moi.

🖱 J'ai un nouveau portable qui a un appareil cinq megapixels.

- Prépayé est plus pratique pour moi.

- J'ai un lecteur MP3 qui est très lèger avec un écran tactile. Je peux facilement télécharger des vidéoclips gratuitement.

- J'envoie des e-mail, je télécharge des vidéoclips et je joue aux jeux.

- Je surfe sur Internet pour trouver des renseignements pour m'aider avec mes devoirs.

- Pour moi, le réseau social est important.

- Les portables sont utiles pour la sécurité.

The disadvantages of new technology – what people say

- Le seul inconvénient, c'est que nous n'avons qu'un ordinateur par classe.

- Malheureusement le système informatique est souvent en panne.

- Les adresses et les sites intéressants disparaissent trop vite.

- Beaucoup de gens passent trop de temps sur leurs ordinateurs.

- On fait moins de sport.

- Il va avoir des problèmes de vue.

> **KEY POINT**
>
> **Vue** means 'eyesight'.

- Il ne s'intéresse qu'à l'ordinateur.

- Il ne joue plus au foot. Il commence à être difficile.

- Il veut manger des fast-food devant l'écran.

- Il devient solitaire, morose même. Les copains n'ont plus d'importance.

- Il est essentiel de limiter l'accès à l'ordinateur.

- Il faut fixer une période déterminée.

- Les portables, sont-ils dangereux pour la santé? Les scientifiques ne sont pas d'accord entre eux. Prudence!

- Cinq millions de minimessages circulent sur les portables chaque jour. Les jeunes écrivent des minimessages pendant les cours. Ils connaissent le clavier par cœur. Ils discutent avec des inconnus. Il faut prendre un faux nom. On ne doit pas donner son adresse ou son numéro.

- C'est moi qui paie la facture.

- On les utilise pour dire n'importe quoi.

- Les gens parlent si fort dans le train. Ça m'ennuie!

- Je me sens surveillé. Ma mère téléphone pour savoir où je suis.

- J'ai perdu mon portable trois fois.

- Beaucoup de personnes utilisent le portable quand ils conduisent. Ça cause beaucoup d'accidents.

- Les appels à l'étranger sont très chers.

- Je ne peux pas vivre sans mon portable, mais à la fin du mois la facture est très chère.

- Dans le train les gens qui parlent au téléphone m'énervent.

- On dit que les portables sont dangereux pour le cerveau.

- Mon baladeur MP3 n'a pas beaucoup de mémoire et je dois recharger les piles tous les jours.

- La fraude est un gros problème.

PROGRESS CHECK

Say or write the following in French:

1. We are soon going to create our own website.
2. Mobiles are very useful to me.
3. You have to set a fixed time period.
4. Friends are no longer important.
5. Be careful!

1. Nous allons bientôt créer notre propre site.
2. Le téléphone portable est très utile pour moi.
3. Il faut fixer une période déterminée.
4. Les copains n'ont plus d'importance.
5. Prudence!

3.4 Grammar

LEARNING SUMMARY

After studying this section, you should be able to understand:

- the plural of nouns
- agreement of adjectives
- irregular feminine forms of adjectives
- the position of adjectives

The plural of nouns

AQA	✓
OCR	✓
EDEXCEL	✓
WJEC	✓
CCEA	✓

As in English, to make some nouns plural in French, you add an **-s**.

| **la chaise** | the chair | ➡ | **les chaises** | the chairs |

Words that end in **-al** change to **-aux** in the plural.

le cheval	the horse	➡	**les chevaux**	the horses
l'animal	the animal	➡	**les animaux**	the animals
le journal	the newspaper	➡	**les journaux**	the newspapers

Words that end in **-eau** add **-x** in the plural.

le cadeau	the present	➡	**les cadeaux**	the presents
le chapeau	the hat	➡	**les chapeaux**	the hats
le château	the castle	➡	**les châteaux**	the castles
l'oiseau	the bird	➡	**les oiseaux**	the birds

Here is a list of other irregular plurals.

le bijou	the jewel	➡	**les bijoux**	the jewels
le fils	the son	➡	**les fils**	the sons
le jeu	the game	➡	**les jeux**	the games
l'œil	the eye	➡	**les yeux**	the eyes

Agreement of adjectives

AQA	✓
OCR	✓
EDEXCEL	✓
WJEC	✓
CCEA	✓

If an adjective describes a feminine singular noun, add **-e**.
If an adjective describes a masculine plural noun, add **-s**.
If an adjective describes a feminine plural noun, add **-es**.

un crayon bleu	a blue pencil
une voiture bleue	a blue car
deux crayons bleus	two blue pencils
deux voitures bleues	two blue cars

If the adjective ends in **-e** already, do not add another **-e**.

un crayon rouge	a red pencil
une voiture rouge	a red car
deux crayons rouges	two red pencils
deux voitures rouges	two red cars

If the adjective ends in **-s** already, do not add another **-s**.

un crayon gris	a grey pencil
deux crayons gris	two grey pencils

Adjectives that end in **-eux** change to **-euse** in the feminine.

un garçon heureux	a happy boy
une fille heureuse	a happy girl
deux garçons heureux	two happy boys
deux filles heureuses	two happy girls

75

Irregular feminine forms of adjectives

AQA ✓
OCR ✓
EDEXCEL ✓
WJEC ✓
CCEA ✓

Masculine singular	Feminine singular	Meaning
beau	belle	beautiful
blanc	blanche	white
bon	bonne	good
cher	chère	expensive, dear
favori	favorite	favourite
frais	fraîche	fresh
gentil	gentille	nice
gros	grosse	big
italien	italienne	Italian
jaloux	jalouse	jealous
long	longue	long
neuf	neuve	brand new
nouveau	nouvelle	new
premier	première	first
secret	secrète	secret
sportif	sportive	athletic
vieux	vieille	old

The position of adjectives

AQA ✓
OCR ✓
EDEXCEL ✓
WJEC ✓
CCEA ✓

Most adjectives come after the noun, e.g. **un livre rouge** not **un rouge livre**.

The following adjectives come before the noun.

beau – beautiful	**jeune** – young	**nouveau** – new
bon – good	**joli** – pretty	**petit** – small
gentil – nice	**long** – long	**premier** – first
grand – big, tall	**mauvais** – bad	**vieux** – old

KEY POINT

Position can change the meaning, e.g. **un cher ami** is 'a dear friend' but **un livre cher** is 'an expensive book'.

PROGRESS CHECK

Say or write the following in French:
1. Horses
2. Eyes
3. A happy girl
4. A jealous woman
5. A beautiful girl
6. Dear Paul

1. Les chevaux 2. Les yeux 3. Une fille heureuse 4. Une femme jalouse 5. Une belle fille 6. Cher Paul

Sample controlled assessment

Speaking

1 🔘 **TRACK 11** You are going to have a conversation with your teacher about what you like doing.

Your teacher will ask about the following and you may have to answer an unexpected question:

- What do you like doing?
- What other sport do you do?
- What other activity do you like?
- **?** An unprepared question (e.g. what is your attitude to reading?)

Teacher: Qu'est-ce que tu aimes faire?

Student: Ce qui me plaît le plus[16] c'est le sport. J'aime tous les sports, mais mon sport favori est le tennis. Je joue au tennis depuis[26] dix ans, c'est-à-dire presque toute ma vie.[16] Mes parents m'ont[32] encouragé(e) parce qu'ils[2] y jouent aussi. J'ai décidé de[4] devenir membre d'un club quand j'avais[13] huit ans et je viens de[20] gagner mon premier tournoi.

Teacher: Tu pratiques un autre sport?

Student: Je suis sur le point de[21] devenir membre d'un club d'équitation. On m'a offert un cheval l'année dernière. Quelle joie![9] C'est le plus beau[23] cheval du monde. Il est si intelligent.[18] J'ai commencé à monter à cheval à l'âge de dix ans, mais j'avais laissé[17] tomber ce sport car je n'avais ni cheval ni argent.[24]

Teacher: Quelle autre activité aimes-tu?

Student: J'adore le cinéma et les films. Le samedi soir, il faut absolument que j'aille[25] au cinéma. Mon frère cadet[16] m'accompagne. Avant d'y aller[6], on cherche les meilleurs films[23] sur Internet. Après avoir trouvé[8] un bon film, on va le voir en ville. Mon frère aime les films d'horreur, tandis que[30] moi je préfère les drames.

Teacher: Tu aimes lire?

Student: Quand j'ai fini mes devoirs le soir, j'ai toujours envie de lire.[1] Sans perdre de temps,[5] je prends mon roman et je lis. Je n'allume jamais[24] la télé. Tant d'émissions[16] sont tellement bêtes![18] Quelle perte de temps![9] Mon frère regarde n'importe quoi[16] à la télé malgré le fait que[19] la plupart des émissions sont stupides...

Turn to page 155 for a translation of this passage.

Turn to page 155 for a translation of this passage.

Examiner's comments

You have to speak for four to six minutes in the controlled assessment. The example given here would take two or three minutes, but you could include holidays as one of the things you like doing and talk for another two minutes or so on that topic (see Chapter 4, pages 86–103). This student is on course for a good grade having implemented most of the 32 points on pages 8–10:

1 An 'avoir' structure
2 A 'parce que' structure
4 'J'ai décidé de...'
5 'Sans' + the infinitive
6 An 'avant de' structure
8 'Après avoir' + the past participle
9 Exclamations
13 An example of the imperfect
16 Impressive vocabulary and structures, e.g. 'ce qui me plaît le plus', 'presque toute ma vie', 'mon frère cadet', 'tant d'émissions', 'n'importe quoi'
17 An example of the pluperfect
18 'Si' and 'tellement' have been used in place of 'très'
19 A 'malgré' structure
20 A 'venir de' structure
21 'Sur le point de'
23 Two examples of the superlative
24 Fine examples of negatives
25 A subjunctive has been used. Brilliant!
26 'Depuis'
30 'Tandis que' is a good connective
32 An example of a pronoun

Sample controlled assessment

Writing

1 Write about the advantages and disadvantages of modern technology. You could include…

- your views on mobile phones
- your views on the Internet
- the disadvantages of ICT
- how the Internet can affect your education.

Ce qui me plaît le plus[16] c'est la sécurité que[30] le portable offre. On n'est jamais[24] seul avec un portable et on peut vraiment facilement[18] téléphoner à la police si on en a besoin.[1] Avant de sortir[6], je dis toujours à mes parents qu'ils[30] peuvent me rejoindre n'importe quand.[16] Cela les[32] rassure. Avec mon nouveau portable, maintenant je peux faire des recherches pour un devoir parce que[2] je peux surfer sur Internet. Pour m'amuser,[31] j'envoie des e-mail, je télécharge des vidéoclips et je joue aux jeux. C'est pratique, cela ne fait pas de bruit et mon portable a un appareil cinq megapixels que[30] je peux utiliser sur les lieux d'un accident ou d'un crime.

Nous avons l'Internet à l'école - c'est génial. C'est un excellent[15] moyen de communiquer avec tout le monde. C'est utile pour contacter des jeunes dans le monde entier. Ça nous aide à trouver des correspondants et ça permet de pratiquer une autre langue. Pour moi, le réseau social est important. J'adore la musique et j'ai un lecteur MP3 qui[30] est si léger, avec un écran tactile.

Mais j'ai décidé[4] qu'il existe des inconvénients. Trop de gens passent trop de temps sur leurs ordinateurs. Ils font moins de sport et après avoir passé[8] tant de temps devant l'écran ils ont des problèmes de vue.[16] Ils ne s'intéressent plus à rien,[24] sauf à l'ordinateur. Ils ont envie de[1] manger des fast-food devant l'écran.[16] Ils commencent à[16] devenir plus solitaires,[22] moroses même.[16] Les copains ne leur sont pas importants. Quel désastre![9] Pour sauver[31] ces gens, il est essentiel de limiter l'accès à l'ordinateur.

Les portables sont dangereux pour la santé. Les scientifiques ne sont pas d'accord entre eux. Prudence! Les jeunes, sans faire attention[5] au professeur, écrivent des minimessages pendant les cours. J'ai une copine qui[30] discute avec un inconnu depuis longtemps. Quelle mauvaise idée![9] J'ai besoin de[1] mon portable, je serais[14] perdu(e) sans lui, mais à la fin du mois la facture est tellement chère.[18]

Turn to page 156 for a translation of this passage.

Examiner's comments

This piece of work, which includes a number of the 32 points on pages 8–10, is of A* quality:

1. 'Avoir' structures
2. Use of 'parce que'
4. 'J'ai décidé…'
5. 'Sans' + the infinitive
6. 'Avant de…'
8. 'Après avoir' + the past participle
9. Exclamations
14. An example of a conditional
15. This is just one example of an adjective
16. Impressive vocabulary and structures, e.g. 'n'importe quand', 'des problèmes de vue', 'l'écran', 'moroses même'
18. 'Vraiment' and 'tellement' have been used in place of 'très'
22. An example of the comparative
24. Excellent negatives
30. 'Que' and 'qui' are good connecting words
31. Examples of 'pour' + the infinitive
32. A good example of a pronoun

Exam practice questions

Listening

1 〔TRACK 12〕 Listen to the phone message that Marie has left for Angélique. Fill in the blanks.

Ce soir on va au .... Avant d'y aller, on se retrouve à la
.... de Michelle à ....h 30. On y va dans la
.... de Michelle. On verra Alain plus .... au café. **(5)**

2 〔TRACK 13〕 Listen to this answerphone message. Fill in the blanks below by choosing the correct number and words from the following options.

03 22 37 56 24	**03 21 38 56 24**	**03 22 38 56 24**	**03 22 38 55 24**

acheter   payer   soirée   concert   restaurant   malade

cadeau   soir   avant-hier   après-demain   boire

Message Téléphonique

Pour: Luc

De: Jean-Paul

Numéro de téléphone: .... – .... – .... – .... – ....

Message:
Jean-Paul est .... et il ne vient pas ce .... Il dit qu'il
viendra .... et qu'il apportera un .... pour Christelle.
Plus tard il veut aller au .... et il va ....! **(7)**

3 〔TRACK 14〕 Listen to these radio extracts. In each case, choose the correct description from the options given and write it in the space provided.

Sport	**Bad weather**	**A politician's visit**	**Road traffic**	**Crime**

(a) ....

(b) ....

(c) ....

(d) ....

(e) .... **(5)**

Exam practice questions

4 TRACK **15** Two people are talking about their likes and dislikes. Tick three boxes for Marc and three boxes for Juliette.

		Marc	Juliette
A	aime rester à la maison	☐	☐
B	n'aime pas les étrangers	☐	☐
C	fait des contacts à l'étranger	☐	☐
D	aime bien sortir	☐	☐
E	déteste les sports	☐	☐
F	adore les sports	☐	☐
G	aime un peu les sports	☐	☐
H	aime la religion	☐	☐
I	aime faire des collections	☐	☐
J	aime danser	☐	☐
K	aime la politique	☐	☐	**(6)**

5 TRACK **16** Listen to this cinema advertisement and complete the information.

(a) Nationality of film ....

(b) Day of premiere ....

(c) Time of premiere ....

(d) Price of ticket ....

(e) Phone number .... **(5)**

6 TRACK **17** Listen to these supermarket announcements. In which department is there a price reduction? Tick the correct box for each announcement.

(a) **A** Cooked meats ☐ **B** Fishmonger's ☐

 C Fruit and vegetables ☐ **D** Chemist's ☐

(b) **A** Men's clothes ☐ **B** Women's clothes ☐

 C Fruit and vegetables ☐ **D** Chemist's ☐

(c) **A** Cooked meats ☐ **B** Fishmonger's ☐

 C Fruit and vegetables ☐ **D** Chemist's ☐ **(3)**

Exam practice questions

7 **TRACK 18** You hear an advert on the radio. Fill in the details (a)–(g).

Name of the restaurant	Restaurant Gilbert
Location	(a) ....
Nationality	(b) ....
Price of the menu of the day	(c) ....
Included in the price is...	(d) ....
Also included is...	(e) ....
The menu of the day is...	(f) ....
Day it closes	(g) ....

(7)

8 **TRACK 19** A French girl is describing what she does on Sunday mornings. Fill in the correct letter in each part of the grid.

A   A walk

B   Lunch

C   Church

D   Exercise

E   Study

F   Shower

G   Breakfast

H   A visit

Time	Activity
7.30	....
8.00	....
8.30	....
9.00	....
10.00	....
11.00	....
11.30	....
12.00	....

(8)

Exam practice questions

Reading

1 Read this advert from the Pays de Landerneau and then **tick the correct boxes**.

VISITEZ LE PAYS TOURISTIQUE DE LANDERNEAU!
Il y a plein de choses à faire!

Ici on peut:
- faire de l'équitation
- faire de l'escrime
- sortir en boîte
- faire de l'escalade

- faire de la planche à voile
- faire de la natation
- faire du parapente
- faire des courses

- aller à la pêche
- faire de la spéléologie
- faire du vélo
- faire du ski nautique

You can:

A  ☐

B  ☐

C ☐

D  ☐

E  ☐

F  ☐

G  ☐

H  ☐

I  ☐

J  ☐

K  ☐

L  ☐

(6)

WJEC Foundation Tier

Exam practice questions

2 Read this article about Leonardo di Caprio from the magazine «Salut!» and **answer the questions**.

Leonardo di Caprio

Il naît le 11 novembre 1974 à Hollywood et fait ses débuts à 14 ans dans les publicités. A ses débuts, ce sont ses parents qui l'ont accompagné aux auditions et qui lui ont fait répéter ses textes.

C'est à l'âge de 17 ans qu'il a entendu parler du projet *Gangs of New York* pour la toute première fois. « A l'époque, ça me semblait être un film parfait pour moi! »

Pour le rôle d'Amsterdam Vallon il a passé une année entière à s'entraîner, à raison de cinq jours par semaine!

Il milite pour la protection des animaux sauvages et il a une passion pour la mode. Son meilleur passe-temps quand il est à Paris, c'est visiter les grandes maisons de mode.

« *Titanic* a changé ma vie. C'est vrai, je ne peux pas me promener dans la rue sans me demander s'il y a un photographe planqué quelque part. Je suis devenu un visage connu et, dès que je vais dans un restaurant, il y a quelqu'un qui téléphone aux journaux. Si je n'avais pas été acteur, j'aurais probablement exercé une profession liée à la biologie ou à l'environnement. »

Example: When was Leonardo born? 1974

(a) What were the first things Leonardo did on screen?

....

(b) How did his parents help him to prepare his parts?

....

(c) How long did he spend preparing for the rôle of Amsterdam Vallon?

....

(d) What cause does di Caprio campaign for?

....

(e) What does he like doing when he goes to Paris?

....

(f) What doesn't he like about being famous?

....

(g) What do people do when they see him in restaurants?

....

(h) What would he have been if he had not become an actor?

.... **(8)**

WJEC Foundation Tier

Exam practice questions

3   Look at the television schedule below.

A la télé ce soir

18.00   **Actualités**

18.30   **Culture**
Monique Dubois discute sa dernière chanson.

19.00   **Ça se discute**
Une interview avec un jeune sans-abri.

19.30   **Marseille/Lyon**
Demi-finale de la coupe.

22.30   **Racines**
Feuilleton. Cette semaine, il y a une dispute entre deux voisins.

23.00   **Meutres dans la nuit**
Meurtre à Paris.

What time is each programme?

Example: News   18.00

(a)   Soap   ....

(b)   Detective story   ....

(c)   Football   ....

(d)   Homelessness   ....

(e)   Music   ....   **(5)**

Exam practice questions

4   These young people are talking about their pocket money.

> Mes parents me donnent 100 euros par mois. Très généreux!
> Avec cet argent je peux aller n'importe où le soir. Je reste
> rarement chez moi le soir.
> *Pierre*

> Le samedi mes parents me donnent 25 euros. Ce n'est pas
> une fortune mais comme ça je peux m'acheter un ou
> deux romans.
> *Jacques*

> Qu'est-ce que je fais de mon argent? C'est facile. J'achète les
> choses qui me plaisent: des bagues, des boucles d'oreille etc.
> *Françoise*

> Mes parents me donnent 50 euros par semaine. C'est assez.
> Le samedi je sors avec mes copains et j'achète des CD. J'en ai
> une vaste collection!
> *Luc*

> Les jupes, les chemisiers, les manteaux. Il faut que j'en
> achète! J'adore les vêtements de mode!   *Jacqueline*

> L'équitation est un sport qui mange tout mon argent. Mais je
> l'adore et je ne fais que ça.
> *Pauline*

> J'adore le dessin. Je dépense tout mon argent en achetant du
> matériel de dessin. Du papier, des crayons etc.   *Edgar*

Write the name of the correct person in each answer space.

(a)   Buys drawing materials   ....

(b)   Buys jewellery   ....

(c)   Likes reading   ....

(d)   Likes going out   ....

(e)   Likes music   ....

(f)   Buys clothes   ....

(g)   Likes horses   ....   **(7)**

4 Holidays

The following topics are covered in this chapter:

- **Holidays and accommodation**
- **Transport**
- **Grammar**

4.1 Holidays and accommodation

LEARNING SUMMARY

After studying this section, you should be able to:

- talk about past and future holidays
- understand information about booking holidays and booking accommodation
- write about experiences abroad

Holidays and accommodation

AQA	✓
OCR	✓
EDEXCEL	✓
WJEC	✓
CCEA	✓

The holiday topic is the topic that lends itself to different tenses. It is the favourite topic for many students in the speaking and writing controlled assessments. The vocabulary sections are particularly important because they are very likely to be tested in the listening and reading exams.

Your controlled speaking assessment must last between four and six minutes. It is a long time to talk about one topic, so why not put two topics together? Your title could be 'The things I like doing'. You could spend two or three minutes speaking about your holidays and two or three minutes speaking about your hobbies (refer to Chapter 3 – Leisure, free time and the media).

Holidays (Les vacances)

l'appareil photo (m) – camera
l'auto-stop (m) – hitch-hiking
Bon voyage! – Have a good trip!
Bon week-end! – Have a good weekend!
la brochure – brochure
le bureau de renseignements – information office
la carte – map
le dépliant – leaflet
la douane – customs
l'étranger (-ère) (m/f) – foreigner
à l'étranger (m) – abroad
l'excursion (f) – trip
le/la guide – guide
le passager – passenger
le passeport – passport

les renseignements (m, pl) – information
la réservation – reservation
le retard – delay
le séjour – stay
le ski – skiing
le souvenir – souvenir
la station de ski – ski resort
le syndicat d'initiative/l'office de tourisme – tourist information office
le tour – tour
la tour – tower
le/la touriste – tourist
le trajet – journey
la valise – suitcase
la visite – visit
le voyage – journey
le voyageur – traveller

l'office de tourisme   la carte   les valises

Camping (Le camping)

l'accueil (m) – welcome, reception
l'allumette (f) – match
le bloc sanitaire – toilet block
le campeur – camper
le camping – campsite
la caravane – caravan
l'eau non-potable (f) – non-drinking water
l'emplacement (m) – pitch

le feu – fire
le matériel – equipment
l'ouvre-boîte (m) – can opener
l'ouvre-bouteille (m) – bottle opener
la pile – (torch) battery
le plat cuisiné – cooked meal
en plein air – in the open air
la salle de jeux – games room
la tente – tent

At the seaside (Au bord de la mer)

le bateau – boat
la marée – tide
la mer – sea

la plage – beach
le port – port
le sable – sand

At the hotel/youth hostel
(À l'hôtel/à l'auberge de jeunesse)

l'ascenseur (m) – lift

les bagages (m, pl) – luggage

la chambre avec un grand lit – room with a double bed

la chambre familiale – family room

la chambre libre – vacant room

la chambre pour deux personnes – double room

la chambre pour une personne – single room

la clé/la clef – key

le dortoir – dormitory

en avance – in advance

la fiche – form

libre – free, vacant

la nationalité – nationality

né(e) le – born on the

le nom – name

le nom de famille – surname

par jour – per day

par personne – per person

la pension (complète) – (full) board

le prénom – first name

la réception – reception

le sac de couchage – sleeping bag

Conversation

AQA ✓
OCR ✓
EDEXCEL ✓
WJEC ✓
CCEA ✓

Où es-tu allé(e) en vacances l'année dernière?

Je suis allé(e) en France.

As-tu visité d'autres pays?

J'ai visité l'Espagne et l'Italie.

Avec qui y es-tu allé(e)?

J'y suis allé(e) avec ma famille.

Quel temps a-t-il fait?

Il a fait beau.

Où as-tu dormi?

On a dormi dans un hôtel.

Combien de temps es-tu resté(e) en France?

Je suis resté(e) deux semaines.

Qu'est-ce que tu as fait?

J'ai nagé et j'ai visité des monuments.

Où iras-tu l'année prochaine?

J'irai en Espagne.

PROGRESS CHECK

Say or write the following in French:

1 I visited Italy.

2 I stayed there for three weeks.

3 I slept in a hotel.

4 The weather was bad.

5 I went to the beach.

6 I swam every day.

1. J'ai visité l'Italie.
2. J'y suis resté(e) trois semaines.
3. J'ai dormi dans un hôtel.
4. Il a fait mauvais.
5. Je suis allé(e) à la plage.
6. J'ai nagé tous les jours.

4.2 Transport

After studying this section, you should be able to:

- take part in controlled speaking assessments about transport
- answer listening and reading questions about how to get to places
- include references to transport in your controlled writing assessments

Travel

AQA	✓
OCR	✓
EDEXCEL	✓
WJEC	✓
CCEA	✓

The following vocabulary will help you in the listening and reading exams, and in the controlled assessment.

Transport (Le transport)

l'aéroport (m) – airport
l'arrêt d'autobus (m) – bus stop
l'autobus (m) – bus
l'autocar (m) – coach
l'autoroute (f) – motorway
l'avion (m) – plane
la bicyclette/le vélo – bicycle
le billet – ticket
le camion – lorry
le car – coach, bus
la destination – destination
la distance – distance
en retard – late
la gare – (railway) station
la gare routière – bus station
le kilomètre – kilometre
le métro – underground train
la moto – motorbike
à pied – on foot
la sortie – exit
la station – tube station
les WC (m, pl) – toilet

l'autobus

l'avion

l'autocar

By car (En voiture)

l'auto (f) – car
la batterie – battery
la carte routière – road map
le coffre – boot (of car)
le conducteur – driver
en panne – broken down
l'essence (f) – petrol
les essuie-glaces (m, pl) – windscreen wipers
le frein – brake
le/la garagiste – garage attendant
le gas-oil – diesel oil
l'huile (f) – oil
la marque – make (i.e. of car)
le moteur – engine
le péage – toll
le permis de conduire – driving licence
le plein – full tank
le pneu – tyre
la pression – pressure (tyres)
réparer – to repair
la roue – wheel
la route – road
la route nationale – main road
sans plomb – unleaded
la station-service – petrol station
le stationnement – parking
la voiture – car

By train (Par le train)

l'aller-retour (m) – return ticket
l'aller-simple (m) – single ticket
le compartiment – compartment
la consigne (automatique) – left luggage (locker)
la correspondance – connection
le départ – departure
direct(e) – direct
la gare – station

occupé(e) – taken
le quai – platform
la salle d'attente – waiting room
SNCF (Société Nationale des Chemins de Fer Français) – French Railways
TGV (Train à Grande Vitesse) – France's high-speed rail service
la voie – track

le péage

les pneus

le train

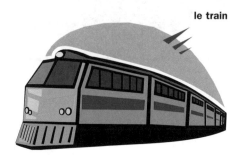

Countries/nationalities (Les pays/nationalités)

l'Autriche

la France

le Royaume-Uni

l'Europe

l'Allemagne

les États-Unis

l'Allemagne (f) – Germany
l'Angleterre (f) – England
l'Autriche (f) – Austria
la Belgique – Belgium
le Canada – Canada
le Danemark – Denmark
l'Écosse (f) – Scotland
l'Espagne (f) – Spain
l'Europe (f) – Europe
les États-Unis (m, pl) – USA
la France – France
la Grande-Bretagne – Great Britain
la Grèce – Greece
la Hollande (f) – Holland
l'Irlande (f) – Ireland
l'Irlande du Nord (f) – Northern Ireland
l'Italie (f) – Italy
le Japon – Japan
le Luxembourg – Luxembourg
le Maroc – Morocco
le pays de Galles – Wales
les Pays-Bas (m, pl) – the Netherlands
le Portugal – Portugal
le Royaume-Uni – United Kingdom
la Russie – Russia

la Suède – Sweden
la Suisse – Switzerland

allemand(e) – German
américain(e) – American
anglais(e) – English
autrichien(ne) – Austrian
belge – Belgian
britannique – British
canadien(ne) – Canadian
danois(e) – Danish
écossais(e) – Scottish
espagnol(e) – Spanish
européen(ne) – European
français(e) – French
gallois(e) – Welsh
grec/grecque – Greek
hollandais(e) – Dutch
irlandais(e) – Irish
italien(ne) – Italian
japonais(e) – Japanese
luxembourgeois(e) – of Luxembourg
marocain(e) – Moroccan
portugais(e) – Portuguese
russe – Russian
suédois(e) – Swedish
suisse – Swiss

Verbs

aller voir – to visit (a person)
arriver – to arrive
attendre – to wait for
se baigner – to bathe
bronzer – to sunbathe
se changer – to change
confirmer – to confirm
coûter – to cost
dépenser – to spend (money)
donner sur – to overlook
dormir – to sleep
envoyer – to send
faire des promenades – to go for walks
faire du camping – to camp
faire le plein – to fill up (with petrol)
loger – to give accommodation
louer – to hire
nager – to swim
partir – to leave
passer – to spend (time)
payer – to pay
pêcher – to fish

prendre des photos – to take photos
se promener – to go for a walk
se renseigner – to get information
réserver – to book
rester – to stay
retourner/revenir – to return
signer – to sign
visiter – to visit (a place)
voyager – to travel

Conversation

AQA ✓
OCR ✓
EDEXCEL ✓
WJEC ✓
CCEA ✓

> **KEY POINT**
>
> Most of the following questions are very predictable, so make sure you have prepared an answer for each one.

1. Your chance to show you can use the perfect tense (see pages 92–93). For maximum marks, try to use a verb that takes 'avoir', a verb that takes 'être' and a reflexive.
2. Your chance to show you can give opinions and justify them.
3. The last part means 'it poured and we were soaked to the skin'.
4. Your chance to show a variety of future tenses (see page 120).

🗣 **Où es-tu allé(e) en vacances l'année dernière et qu'est-ce que tu as fait?[1]**
💬 Je suis allé(e) en France avec ma famille. J'ai fait beaucoup de choses. J'ai nagé, j'ai lu, je suis allé(e) à Paris, j'ai bronzé et j'ai dansé.
🗣 **Tu aimes la France?[2]**
💬 J'adore la France parce que j'aime la cuisine, les gens et surtout le climat.
🗣 **Quel temps a-t-il fait?**
💬 Il a fait beau la plupart du temps, mais un jour il a plu à verse et on a été trempé jusqu'aux os![3]
🗣 **Comment as-tu voyagé en France?**
💬 On a voyagé en voiture. On a pris le bateau à Douvres. Le voyage a duré quinze heures.
🗣 **Où iras-tu l'année prochaine et qu'est-ce que tu feras?[4]**
💬 J'irai en France encore une fois avec ma famille. Je bronzerai, je nagerai, je danserai, je lirai et je me reposerai.
🗣 **Comment voyageras-tu en France?**
💬 Je voyagerai en voiture et en bateau.

4.3 Grammar

LEARNING SUMMARY	**After studying this section, you should be able to understand:** ● the perfect tense

The perfect tense

AQA	✓
OCR	✓
EDEXCEL	✓
WJEC	✓
CCEA	✓

The perfect is the tense you use to say what you did in the past, e.g. I went to town and I bought some clothes.

Verbs conjugated with avoir

To form most verbs in the perfect tense, you need to use the correct form of the present tense of **avoir**.

-er verbs	-ir verbs	-re verbs
donner	finir	vendre
j'ai donné	**j'ai fini**	**j'ai vendu**
(I have given, I gave)	(I have finished, I finished)	(I have sold, I sold)
tu as donné	**tu as fini**	**tu as vendu**
il a donné	**il a fini**	**il a vendu**
elle a donné	**elle a fini**	**elle a vendu**
nous avons donné	**nous avons fini**	**nous avons vendu**
vous avez donné	**vous avez fini**	**vous avez vendu**
ils ont donné	**ils ont fini**	**ils ont vendu**
elles ont donné	**elles ont fini**	**elles ont vendu**

The following verbs have irregular past participles.

avoir	➡	**j'ai eu**	I had, I have had
boire	➡	**j'ai bu**	I drank, I have drunk
connaître	➡	**j'ai connu**	I knew, I have known
courir	➡	**j'ai couru**	I ran, I have run
croire	➡	**j'ai cru**	I believed, I have believed
devoir	➡	**j'ai dû**	I had to (owed), I have had to (have owed)

dire	➡	j'ai dit	I said, I have said
écrire	➡	j'ai écrit	I wrote, I have written
être	➡	j'ai été	I was, I have been
faire	➡	j'ai fait	I made/did, I have made/done
lire	➡	j'ai lu	I read, I have read
mettre	➡	j'ai mis	I put, I have put
ouvrir	➡	j'ai ouvert	I opened, I have opened
pleuvoir	➡	il a plu	it rained, it has rained
pouvoir	➡	j'ai pu	I was able, I have been able
prendre	➡	j'ai pris	I took, I have taken
recevoir	➡	j'ai reçu	I received, I have received
rire	➡	j'ai ri	I laughed, I have laughed
savoir	➡	j'ai su	I knew, I have known
suivre	➡	j'ai suivi	I followed, I have followed
vivre	➡	j'ai vécu	I lived, I have lived
voir	➡	j'ai vu	I saw, I have seen
vouloir	➡	j'ai voulu	I wanted, I have wanted

Verbs conjugated with être

A small number of common verbs use the verb **être** to form the perfect tense. These verbs are sometimes easier to remember in pairs.

entrer

aller	to go	**rentrer**	to go back	**naître**	to be born
venir	to come	**retourner**	to return	**mourir**	to die
arriver	to arrive	**descendre**	to go down	**devenir**	to become
partir	to leave	**monter**	to go up	**revenir**	to come back
entrer	to enter	**rester**	to stay		
sortir	to go out	**tomber**	to fall		

The following verbs have irregular past participles.

revenir	➡	je suis revenu(e)	I came back, I have come back
venir	➡	je suis venu(e)	I came, I have come
mourir	➡	il est mort, elle est morte	he died, she died
naître	➡	je suis né(e)	I was born

Reflexive verbs

With reflexive verbs, you use **être**.

se laver	
je me suis lavé(e) (I washed myself)	**nous nous sommes lavé(e)s**
tu t'es lavé(e)	**vous vous êtes lavé(e)(s)**
il s'est lavé	**ils se sont lavés**
elle s'est lavée	**elles se sont lavées**

PROGRESS CHECK

Say or write the following in French:

1 I went to the restaurant. I ate a steak and I drank a glass of beer.

1. Je suis allé(e) au restaurant. J'ai mangé un steak et j'ai bu un verre de bière.

Sample controlled assessment

Speaking

1 TRACK **20** You are discussing last year's holiday with a French friend. Your teacher will play the part of the friend. You will be asked about the following:

- What you did for your holidays last year
- What the weather was like
- What the journey to your holiday destination was like
- Your overall impressions
- **?** An unprepared question (e.g. your holiday plans for next year).

Student: L'année dernière, j'ai décidé de[4] partir en vacances au mois de juin avec mon frère aîné.[16] Je voulais[13] rendre visite à mes amis en Suisse. Ils y habitent depuis[26] deux ans. Quelle bonne idée![9] Je pense que la Suisse est le plus beau pays du monde parce que le paysage et les montagnes sont super![3]

Teacher: Quel temps faisait-il?

Student: Il faisait beau et nous sommes allés à l'aéroport en taxi. Nous sommes montés dans l'avion, j'ai mis ma ceinture de sécurité et l'avion a décollé. Je n'avais pas peur.[1]

Teacher: Qu'est-ce que tu as fait pendant le vol?

Student: Avant de partir,[6] j'avais acheté[17] un roman. J'ai joué aux cartes et j'ai lu. Nous avons déjeuné, mais le repas n'était pas très bon. C'était du poulet, et je ne l'ai pas aimé. Après avoir mangé,[8] je ne me sentais pas bien.[13] Je suis arrivé(e) en Suisse à six heures du soir et mes amis m'attendaient à l'aéroport. Ils étaient très sympa. En allant à la maison, nous avons traversé la ville de Genève, nous avons admiré le lac, et plus tard, nous sommes arrivés chez eux. En arrivant,[7] nous avons dîné. Le repas était délicieux. Puis nous nous sommes couchés.

Teacher: Et tes impressions?

Student: Je pense que le voyage s'est très bien passé et que mes amis sont très gentils.

Teacher: Que feras-tu l'année prochaine?

Student: Il faut que je retourne[25] en Suisse pour skier.[31] Je voudrais faire du ski parce que[2] j'adore faire du ski et la neige est si bonne[18] à Verbier. Je voudrais aussi monter à cheval parce que[2] j'ai un cheval ici en Angleterre et que j'aime bien faire de l'équitation malgré la neige.[19] L'année dernière à Verbier, j'ai fait des promenades dans les montagnes et je voudrais faire la même chose cette année puisque[30] ça m'a vraiment plu. Il y a une patinoire et une piscine à Verbier.

Turn to page 156 for a translation of this passage.

Turn to page 156 for a translation of this passage.

Examiner's comments

This student has boosted his/her grade by including a number of the 32 mark-winning points outlined on pages 8–10:

1   An 'avoir' structure
2   Two examples of the use of 'parce que'
3   A fine example of a justified point of view
4   'J'ai décidé de…'
6   An 'avant de' structure
7   'En' + the present participle
8   'Après avoir' + the past participle
9   An exclamation
13 Two examples of the imperfect tense
16 Excellent vocabulary used here
17 An example of the pluperfect tense
18 'Si' is used here rather than 'très'
19 'Malgré'
25 A subjunctive has been included!
26 A 'depuis' structure
30 'Puisque' is a good connective
31 'Pour' + the infinitive

Sample controlled assessment

Writing

1 Write about a recent holiday. You could include…

- the destination
- who you went with
- your plans for this summer.
- the accommodation
- your overall opinion

Je vais te décrire mon séjour à Blackpool. J'étais logé dans un hôtel quatre étoiles. C'était super parce que la piscine était toujours vide! Le matin, je me promenais le long de la plage: l'après-midi, je jouais au foot dans le parc et le soir je sortais avec mes parents. Un jour, je suis allé à un parc d'attractions. C'était affreux parce que les files d'attente étaient très longues.

À mon avis, le séjour était excellent parce que nous nous sommes bien amusés tout le temps. Il faisait un temps superbe tous les jours. Cet été, j'irai aux États-Unis et je verrai tous les monuments historiques. Je voudrais voir New York.

Now compare the piece of work above with the following passage.

Je vais te[32] décrire[12] mon séjour à Blackpool. Je viens d'y[20] passer deux semaines inoubliables.[16] Pour moi, Blackpool est la meilleure ville d'Angleterre pour les vacances parce qu'il[2] y a toujours quelque chose à faire.[3] J'étais logé dans un hôtel cinq étoiles parce que[2] mes parents avaient gagné[17] à la loterie. C'était super parce que[2] la piscine était[13] toujours vraiment vide![18] Quel luxe![9] Ils ont gagné une fortune donc maintenant on a acheté une voiture super et on loge dans les meilleurs hôtels.[16] Heureusement,[16] ma sœur cadette[16] a refusé de nous[32] accompagner parce qu'elle[2] n'aime pas Blackpool. Elle est allée rendre visite à ma grand-mère. Le matin, je me promenais[13] le long de la plage. L'après-midi, je jouais[13] au foot dans le parc et le soir je sortais[13] avec mes parents. Il faut que je fasse[25] beaucoup d'exercice pour me maintenir[31] en bonne condition.

Un jour, j'ai décidé d'aller[4] à un parc d'attractions. En arrivant,[7] j'ai vu les files d'attente.[16] C'était affreux parce que[2] les files étaient tellement longues.[18] Après avoir attendu[8] deux heures, je n'étais pas content(e). J'étais sur le point de[21] demander un remboursement. Je n'irai plus[24] aux parcs d'attractions.

À mon avis, le séjour était excellent parce que nous nous sommes bien amusés tout le temps et j'ai eu la chance de faire la connaissance d'un beau garçon/d'une belle jeune fille.[3] Je suis sorti(e) avec lui/elle et on s'est bien entendus. Il faisait un temps superbe tous les jours. J'y retournerais[14] sans hésiter[5] malgré[19] les longues files d'attente.

Cet été, j'irai aux États-Unis et je verrai mon frère aîné.[16] Il habite là depuis deux ans.[26] Je voudrais voir New York et il m'accompagnera. J'ai envie de[1] traverser le pays pour mieux le connaître. Mon frère louera une voiture et on partira!

Turn to page 156 for a translation of this passage.

Turn to page 156 for a translation of this passage.

Examiner's comments

The first version is too short and has few mark-winning structures. It would not get a high grade. The second passage is about the right length and uses most of the 32 points on pages 8–10, making it worth an A*:

1 An 'avoir' structure
2 'Parce que' structures
3 Justified points of view
4 'J'ai décidé de…'
5 'Sans' + the infinitive
7 'En' + the present participle
8 'Après avoir' + the past participle
9 An exclamation
12 An example of the future tense
13 Several examples of the imperfect tense
14 A conditional has been included
16 Impressive vocabulary and structures, e.g. 'inoubliables', 'les meilleurs hôtels', 'heureusement', 'ma sœur cadette', 'les files d'attente', 'mon frère aîné'
17 An example of the pluperfect
18 Examples of the use of 'vraiment' and 'tellement'
19 'Malgré'
20 A 'venir de' structure
21 'Sur le point de'
24 A good example of a negative
25 A subjunctive has been included
26 A 'depuis' structure
31 'Pour' + the infinitive
32 Good examples of a pronoun

Exam practice questions

Listening

1 TRACK 21 — You are at a railway station in France. Listen to the following train announcement.

(a) At what platform and at what time does the train arrive?

(i) What platform? ....

(ii) What time? ....

(b) What can you do on the train? **Tick two boxes**.

A Sleep ☐

B Eat ☐

C Use a computer ☐

D Take your bike ☐ **(4)**

WJEC Foundation Tier

2 TRACK 22 — You are on holiday in France and are in front of a museum. You hear an announcement.

(a) On what day can you have a guided tour of the museum? ....

(b) At what time? ....

(c) Where can you buy your ticket? ....

(d) How long will the guided tour last? .... **(4)**

3 TRACK 23 — A woman is describing her impressions of Spain. Tick the correct box in each case.

(a)

Favourable ☐
Unfavourable ☐

(b)

Favourable ☐
Unfavourable ☐

(c)

Favourable ☐
Unfavourable ☐

(d)

Favourable ☐
Unfavourable ☐

Exam practice questions

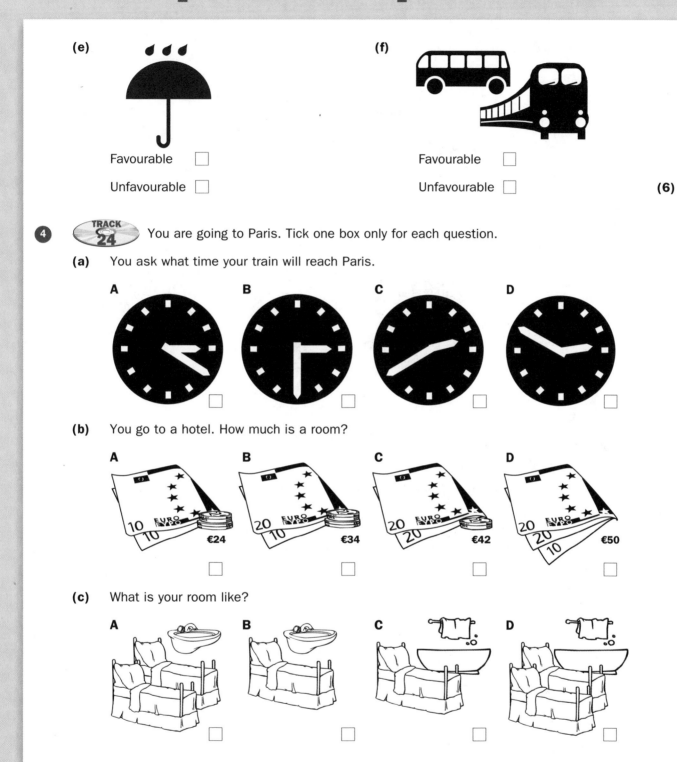

(e)

Favourable ☐

Unfavourable ☐

(f)

Favourable ☐

Unfavourable ☐

(6)

4 TRACK 24 You are going to Paris. Tick one box only for each question.

(a) You ask what time your train will reach Paris.

A ☐ B ☐ C ☐ D ☐

(b) You go to a hotel. How much is a room?

A €24 ☐ B €34 ☐ C €42 ☐ D €50 ☐

(c) What is your room like?

A ☐ B ☐ C ☐ D ☐

Exam practice questions

(d) How should you go to the town centre?

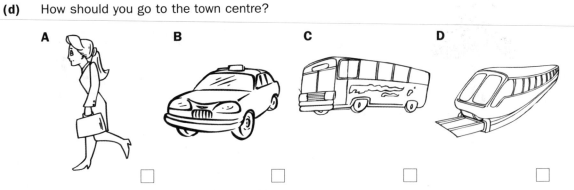

A ☐   B ☐   C ☐   D ☐

(e) What should you see in the town centre?

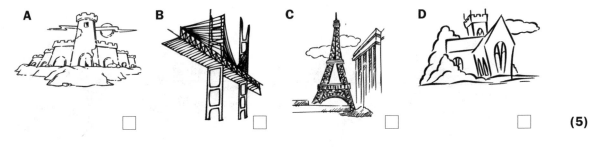

A ☐   B ☐   C ☐   D ☐

(5)

5 TRACK 25   Sandra is describing her holidays.

(a) The campsite is located in ....

(b) Why did she choose that campsite? Tick the correct box.

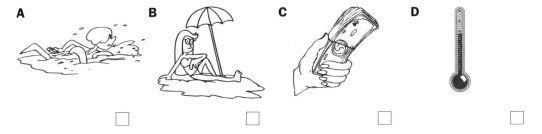

A ☐   B ☐   C ☐   D ☐

(c) What did Sandra prefer? Tick the correct box.

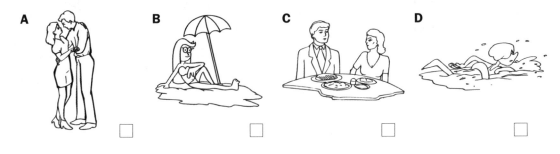

A ☐   B ☐   C ☐   D ☐

Exam practice questions

(d) How did she get there? Tick the correct box.

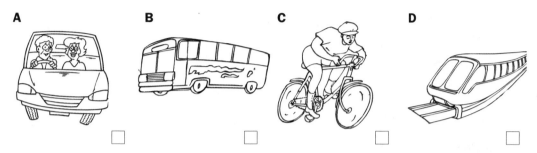

A   B   C   D

☐   ☐   ☐   ☐

(e) What was the weather like? Tick the correct box.

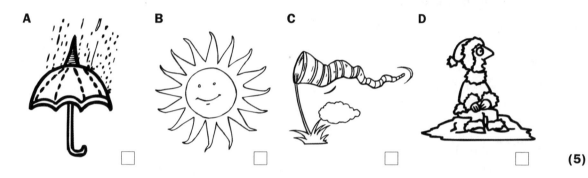

A   B   C   D

☐   ☐   ☐   ☐   **(5)**

6 **TRACK 26** A father and a mother are discussing their trip to London. Tick the correct boxes to show which person is expressing each opinion.

	The mother	The father
(a) This person wants to go by car.	☐	☐
(b) This person never gets seasick.	☐	☐
(c) This person does not like to eat on the ferry.	☐	☐
(d) This person likes to see the countryside.	☐	☐
(e) This person wants to go by plane.	☐	☐
(f) This person wants to go directly to the hotel.	☐	☐
(g) This person suggests going by train.	☐	☐
(h) This person says the trains are sometimes late.	☐	☐
(i) This person says the train will take them near their hotel.	☐	☐

(9)

Exam practice questions

7 TRACK **27** Listen to this radio advertisement about a weekend in Spain. Write the answers in English.

A trip to Madrid

(a)   Length of the flight: ....

(b)   Price of the flight: ....

(c)   Not included in the offer: ....

(d)   Problem with the hotels: ....

(e)   Solution to this problem: ....

(f)   Time of dinner in Spain: ....

(g)   The best dish: ....

(h)   Method of payment: .... **(8)**

8 TRACK **28** A group of French students is spending a week in London and each student is asked by one of their teachers for their impressions of the city. Listen to what each student says and decide which statement from the list best describes his or her opinion. Write after each name the letter of the matching statement. You will not use all the letters. The students are interviewed in the order given.

A Is not very impressed

B Likes it a lot

C Finds it very like Paris

D Dislikes the noise and the pollution

E Is impressed by the number of things to visit

F Finds it friendly

(a)   Carine ....

(b)   François ....

(c)   Stéphanie ....

(d)   Caroline ....

(e)   Christophe .... **(5)**

Exam practice questions

Reading

1 Read the e-mail message below.

> Monsieur
>
> Je vous remercie de votre email et j'ai réservé les chambres que vous désirez. Notre hôtel se trouve dans un faubourg à un kilomètre du centre-ville. Nous avons un grand parking. Si vous arrivez en car, prenez un taxi: ce n'est pas cher. Les chambres sont au deuxième étage et nous n'avons pas d'ascenseur. Le petit déjeuner n'est pas compris dans le prix.
>
> A bientôt
> Le propriétaire

Choose the appropriate words from the box below to complete the sentences that follow.

peu	annulé	garer	payer	l'escalier
mairie	supplément	taxe	centre-ville	réservé

(a) Le propriétaire a .... des chambres.

(b) L'hôtel ne se trouve pas au ....

(c) On peut .... la voiture à l'hôtel.

(d) Un taxi est .... cher.

(e) Pour aller aux chambres il faut prendre ....

(f) Pour le petit déjeuner il faut payer un ....   **(6)**

2 You are on holiday with your family in France and are travelling by car. Answer the following questions about signs you see.

(a) You are looking for somewhere to park and see this sign.

> **P** STATIONNEMENT PAYANT
>
> OUVERT DE 8ʰ A 18ʰ
> TOUS LES JOURS
> SAUF DIMANCHES
> ET JOUR FERIES
>
> PRENEZ UN TICKET ↓

    (i) What kind of car park is it?

    .... **(1)**

    (ii) What are the opening times? .... **(1)**

    (iii) Which days is it open? .... **(3)**

    (iv) What do you have to do? .... **(1)**

(b) Later, you see this sign. Why are you not allowed to park here?

> SORTIE POMPIERS

.... **(1)**

(c) Finally, you see this sign. Where is this car park?

> **Parking**
> devant l'hôtel de ville

.... **(1)**

Exam practice questions

3 Read the e-mail message below, then answer the questions that follow.

> Peter
>
> J'ai une bonne nouvelle! Tu veux venir en France cet été? Mon oncle vient de nous inviter à passer deux semaines dans son camping. Il est propriétaire d'un grand camping près de Toulouse.
>
> On devra aider avec le travail. Il faudra vider les poubelles, servir dans le magasin et nettoyer les tentes. Et avec les campeurs britanniques tu devras traduire. Toulouse est très animée et il y a beaucoup d'étudiants. En plus l'Espagne n'est pas loin et on peut louer une voiture. Envoie un minimessage pour me dire ton opinion. Ce sera super.
>
> Jacques.

(a) Why has Jacques e-mailed? .... **(1)**

(b) Who owns the campsite? .... **(1)**

(c) How long have they been invited for? .... **(1)**

(d) List three ways in which they can help at the campsite.

   (i) ....

   (ii) ....

   (iii) .... **(3)**

(e) What special task will Peter have? .... **(1)**

(f) Why is Toulouse a lively city? .... **(1)**

(g) **(i)** Where does Jacques hope to go? ....

   (ii) By what means of transport? .... **(2)**

(h) What must Peter do to reply? .... **(1)**

Exam practice questions

4 Read these hotel advertisements.

A

Hôtel de la Mer

à 100 mètres de la plage
TV. ascenseur
garages
bar, salons
39 chambres tout confort.

mars – octobre

hoteldelamer.fr

Tel: 02 96 27 27 29
Fax: 02 96 22 23 29

B

Hôtel Luc

garages
bar, salons
32 chambres tout confort.
Ouvert toute l'année

~ h o t e l l u c . f r ~

Tel: 02 96 75 73 49
Fax: 02 96 78 62 41

C

HÔTEL CASPIN

- garages
- bar, salons
- 42 chambres tout confort.
- mars – novembre
- TV avec chaînes anglaises

hotelcaspin.fr

Tel: 02 96 54 12 08
Fax: 02 96 56 17 31

D

Hôtel Accueil

situé dans un château du XVIIe siècle
garages
bar, salons
45 chambres tout confort toutes
avec cuisine.

mars – septembre

hotelaccueil.fr
Tel: 02 96 86 67 01
Fax: 02 96 83 64 06

Write the letter of the best hotel to stay at if you…

(a) are interested in history. ....

(b) need a lift to get to your room. ....

(c) want to see your favourite soap. ....

(d) want to go in winter. ....

(e) want to cook your own meals. ....

(f) want to be near the beach. .... **(6)**

5 Home, local area and environment

The following topics are covered in this chapter:

- Special occasions celebrated in the home
- Home and local area
- The environment
- Grammar

5.1 Special occasions celebrated in the home

LEARNING SUMMARY	**After studying this section, you should be able to:**
	• describe different special occasions
	• say how you celebrate special occasions

Special occasions

AQA	✓
OCR	✓
EDEXCEL	✓
WJEC	✓
CCEA	✓

You need to study the vocabulary and know the French for special occasions like Christmas and Easter. These may well appear in your reading and listening exams. You might like to use a special occasion for your controlled writing or speaking assessment.

Celebrations (Les célébrations)

Aid – Eid
l'arbre de Noël – Christmas tree
Bon anniversaire! – Happy birthday!
Bonne année! – Happy New Year!
Diwali – Diwali
la fête nationale – Bastille Day
Hannoukah – Hanukkah
Le jour de l'an – New Year's Day
Joyeux Noël! – Happy Christmas!
le mariage – wedding
Meilleurs voeux! – Best wishes!

la naissance – birth
Noël – Christmas
le nouvel an – New Year
le nouvel an chinois – Chinese New Year
Pâques – Easter
le père Noël – Father Christmas
le quatorze juillet – July 14
Le Ramadan – Ramadan
la Saint-Sylvestre – New Year's Eve
la veille de Noël – Christmas Eve

Conversation starters

À Noël,	on envoie...	– we send...
Au jour de l'an,	on offre...	– we give...
Le quatorze juillet,	on décore...	– we decorate...
À Diwali,	on chante...	– we sing...
À la fin du Ramadan,	on danse...	– we dance...
À Hannoukah,	on fête...	– we celebrate...
Au nouvel an chinois,	on jeûne...	– we fast...
	on mange...	– we eat...
	on boit ...	– we drink...
	on allume...	– we light...
	on souhaite...	– we wish...

Useful phrases

On achète des cadeaux.

We buy presents.

On envoie des cartes.

We send cards.

On décore la maison.

We decorate the house.

On mange beaucoup.

We eat a lot.

On reçoit des cartes et des cadeaux.

We get cards and presents.

Il y a un défilé et le soir il y a un bal dans la rue avec des feux d'artifice.

There is a procession and in the evening there is an open-air dance
with fireworks.

> **KEY POINT**
>
> The sentence above refers to Bastille Day (July 14) in France.

On offre des cadeaux.

We give presents.

On allume la maison.

We put up lights outside the house.

On mange des choses sucrées.

We eat sweet things.

On allume des bougies.

We light candles.

On joue aux jeux.

We play games.

On mange des crêpes et des beignets.

We eat pancakes and doughnuts.

On fait le réveillon au nouvel an.

We have a New Year's Eve party.

On se couche très tard.

We go to bed very late.

5.2 Home and local area

LEARNING SUMMARY

After studying this section, you should be able to:
- describe your home
- say what you do at home
- talk about your town, neighbourhood and region
- give and understand directions
- describe the weather and understand a weather forecast

Home

AQA	✓
OCR	✓
EDEXCEL	✗
WJEC	✓
CCEA	✓

The following vocabulary will help you in the listening and reading exams. In the controlled speaking assessment, you may be asked to talk for a minute or two about your home, describing the rooms and the garden. You need to be able to talk in the perfect tense about what you did at home and in the future tense about what you will do there. A popular choice for the controlled writing or speaking assessments is to describe your ideal home.

Around the home (À la maison)

la lampe

l'appartement (m) – flat, apartment	**le meuble** – furniture
la boîte aux lettres – letterbox	**meublé** – furnished
la chaise – chair	**la moquette** – (fitted) carpet
le chauffage (central) – central heating	**le placard** – cupboard
chez moi – to/at my house	**le plafond** – ceiling
le code postal – postcode	**le plancher** – floor
l'escalier (m) – stairs	**la poubelle** – dustbin
l'étagère (f) – shelf	**le rideau** – curtain
la fenêtre – window	**la table** – table
l'horloge (f) – clock	**le tiroir** – drawer
la lampe – lamp	**le toit** – roof
le lavabo – washbasin	**le volet** – shutter
la lumière – light	**le WC** – toilet

Materials (Les matières)

le coton – cotton	**le métal** – metal
le cuir – leather	**le nylon** – nylon
la laine – wool	**le plastique** – plastic

la poussière

Housework (Le ménage)

l'aspirateur (m) – vacuum cleaner	**la poussière** – dust
la lessive – washing powder	**la tache** – stain
le linge – linen, washing	**la vaisselle** – washing-up

Verbs

aider – to help	**faire le repassage** – to do the ironing
arroser – to water	**mettre la table** – to lay the table
bricoler – to do DIY	**mettre le couvert** – to lay the table
débarrasser la table – to clear the table	**nettoyer** – to clean
faire la vaisselle – to do the washing-up	**ranger** – to tidy
faire le jardinage – to do the gardening	**sécher** – to dry
faire le lit – to make the bed	**stationner** – to park
faire le ménage – to do the housework	**travailler** – to work

le fauteuil

la chaîne-stéréo

The living room (Le séjour/La salle de séjour)

la bibliothèque – bookcase	**le lecteur de DVD** – DVD player
le buffet – sideboard	**le magnétoscope** – video recorder
le canapé – settee	**la peinture** – painting
la chaîne hi-fi – stereo	**la platine laser** – CD player
la chaîne-stéréo – stereo	**la radio** – radio
la cheminée – fireplace	**le tableau** – painting
le fauteuil – armchair	**la télévision** – TV

The bedroom (La chambre)

l'armoire (f) – wardrobe	**le lit** – bed
la commode – chest of drawers	**l'ordinateur (m)** – computer
la couverture – blanket	**l'oreiller (m)** – pillow
le drap – sheet	**le réveil** – alarm clock

la brosse à dents

The bathroom (La salle de bains)

la baignoire – bath(tub)
la brosse à dents – toothbrush
les ciseaux (m, pl) – scissors
le dentifrice – toothpaste
la douche – shower
le miroir – mirror

le rasoir – razor
le robinet – tap
le savon – soap
la serviette – towel
le shampooing – shampoo

The kitchen (La cuisine)

la casserole – saucepan
le congélateur – freezer
la cuisinière à gaz – gas cooker
la cuisinière électrique – electric cooker
l'évier (m) – sink
faire la cuisine – to cook
le four à micro-ondes – microwave oven

le frigidaire – fridge
le frigo – fridge
le lave-vaisselle – dishwasher
la machine à laver/le lave-linge – washing machine
le plateau – tray

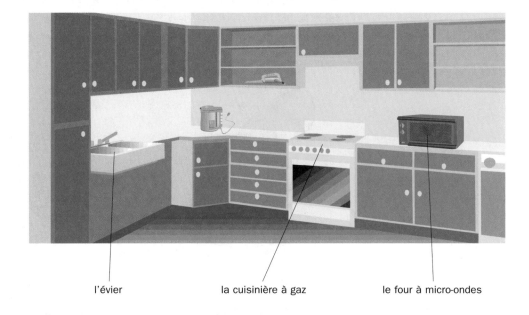

l'évier   la cuisinière à gaz   le four à micro-ondes

The garden (Le jardin)

l'arbre (m) – tree
la branche – branch
la feuille – leaf
la fleur – flower

la haie – hedge
l'herbe (f) – grass
la pelouse – lawn
la plante – plant

l'arbre   **la feuille**   **la fleur**

Adjectives

clair(e) – clear, light
confortable – comfortable
électrique – electric
moderne – modern

neuf (neuve) – new
pittoresque – picturesque
typique – typical

PROGRESS CHECK

Say or write the following in French:
1. Where is the letterbox?
2. We have modern furniture.
3. I love cooking.
4. We have bought a freezer.
5. Yesterday I did the washing-up.
6. This evening I will cook the dinner.

6. Ce soir je préparerai le repas.
5. Hier j'ai fait la vaisselle.
4. Nous avons acheté un congélateur.
3. J'adore faire la cuisine.
2. Nous avons des meubles modernes.
1. Où est la boîte aux lettres?

Conversation: Grades G–D

AQA	✓
OCR	✓
EDEXCEL	X
WJEC	✓
CCEA	✓

You need to be able to answer the following questions without thinking. The longer your answers, the more marks you will get. If you give very short answers or answers without a verb, you will lose marks.

🔵 **Tu habites une maison ou un appartement?**
⚪ **J'habite une maison.**
🔵 **Comment est ta maison?**
⚪ **Elle est jolie et confortable.**
🔵 **À quelle distance se trouve ta maison du collège?**
⚪ **Elle se trouve à un kilomètre du collège.**
🔵 **Combien de pièces y a-t-il?**
⚪ **Il y en a six.[1]**
🔵 **Qu'est-ce que tu vois de la fenêtre de ta maison?**
⚪ **Je vois les maisons de mes voisins, des voitures et des bâtiments.[2]**
🔵 **Qu'est-ce qu'il y a dans ton jardin?**
⚪ **Il y a des fleurs et des arbres.**
🔵 **Qu'est-ce qu'il y a dans ta chambre?**
⚪ **Il y a un lit, une table et une chaise.**

1 You could name the rooms and get more marks.
2 Add a few more details!

Conversation: Grades C–A*

AQA	✓
OCR	✓
EDEXCEL	✗
WJEC	✓
CCEA	✓

Remember to…

- use long sentences
- justify your opinions
- use past, present and future tenses
- give opinions.

Décris ta maison.

Ma maison est très jolie. Il y a trois chambres, une cuisine, une salle à manger, une salle de séjour et une salle de bains.[1]

Décris ta chambre.

Ma chambre est très confortable. Il y a un lit,[2] une chaise, une table, une télé et beaucoup de livres.

Qu'est-ce que tu fais dans ta chambre?[3]

Je fais mes devoirs, je lis, j'écoute de la musique, je regarde la télé et bien sûr je dors.

Qu'est-ce que tu as fait dans ta chambre hier soir?[4]

Hier soir, j'ai lu mon livre, j'ai écouté de la musique, j'ai regardé la télé, j'ai joué avec l'ordinateur et j'ai dormi.[5]

Et ce soir, qu'est-ce que tu vas faire chez toi?[6]

Je lirai mon livre, j'écouterai de la musique, je regarderai la télé, je jouerai avec l'ordinateur et je dormirai.

Tu aimes ta maison?[7]

À mon avis, ma maison est une maison parfaite parce qu'il y a un grand jardin, que les voisins sont sympa et qu'elle se trouve près du centre-ville.

Décris ton jardin.

Je ne travaille pas dans le jardin parce que je déteste le jardinage. Mais mes parents ont planté beaucoup de fleurs et l'an prochain ils vont cultiver des légumes.[8]

1 Add more details.

2 So far so good but the only verb forms so far are 'il y a' and 'est'.

3 An opportunity to vary your structures. With an open question like this, make sure you give back at least five verbs.

4 A chance to use the perfect. Remember: at least four examples.

5 You have not used a verb that takes 'être'. You could add 'je suis resté(e) dans ma chambre toute la soirée'.

6 A chance to use the future (see page 120).

7 Your chance to give an opinion. Start with 'À mon avis…'.

8 Three tenses in one answer!

Town, neighbourhood and region

AQA	✓
OCR	✓
EDEXCEL	✓
WJEC	✓
CCEA	✓

The following vocabulary will help you in the listening and reading exams. In your controlled speaking or writing assessment, you may be asked to describe your town or region. Weather is often tested in the listening and reading exams.

The environment (L'environnement)

le bois – wood
la campagne – countryside
le champ – field
le chemin – path, way
la colline – hill
l'étoile (f) – star
la forêt – forest
le lac – lake

la mer – sea
la montagne – mountain
le pays – country
la région – region
la rivière – river
le verger – orchard
le village – village
la ville – town, city

le chemin

la montagne

la rivière

Animals (Les animaux)

le cheval – horse
le cochon – pig
l'insecte (m) – insect

le mouton – sheep
l'oiseau (m) – bird
la poule – hen

le poulet – chicken
la souris – mouse
la vache – cow

le cheval

l'oiseau

la souris

Colours (Les couleurs)

blanc (m)/blanche (f) – white
bleu – blue
brun – dark brown
gris – grey

jaune – yellow
marron – brown
noir – black
pâle – pale
rose – pink

rosé – pinkish
rouge – red
roux (rousse) – reddish-brown
vert – green

Compass points and directions (Les points cardinaux et les directions)

l'est (m) – east

le nord – north

l'ouest (m) – west

le sud – south

à droite – to/on the right

en bas – below, downstairs

en haut – above, upstairs

entouré de – surrounded by

en face de – opposite

à gauche – to/on the left

là – there

là-bas – over there

loin de – far from

où – where

Pour aller à…? – How do I get to…?

près de – near

tout droit – straight on

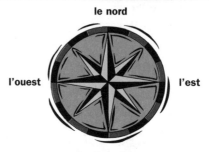

le nord

l'ouest   l'est

le sud

Adjectives

ancien(ne) – former, ancient

confortable – comfortable

moderne – modern

neuf (neuve) – new

pittoresque – picturesque

typique – typical

les nuages

la pluie

l'orage

The weather (Le temps)

l'averse (f) – shower (of rain)

le brouillard – fog

la brume – mist

la chaleur – heat

le ciel – sky

le climat – climate

le degré – degree

l'éclair (m) – flash of lightning

la glace – ice

la météo – weather forecast

la neige – snow

le nuage – cloud

l'orage (m) – storm

la pluie – rain

le soleil – sun

la température – temperature

la tempête – storm

le tonnerre – thunder

le vent – wind

Weather verbs

briller – to shine
il fait beau/chaud/froid/du vent – it is nice/hot/cold/windy

il gèle/neige/pleut – it is freezing/snowing/raining

In the street (Dans la rue)

le bruit – noise
le carrefour – crossroads
le centre-ville – town-centre
la circulation – traffic
le coin – corner
l'embouteillage (m) – traffic jam
les feux – traffic lights
le passage à niveau – level crossing
le passage clouté – pedestrian crossing

le passant – passer-by
le piéton – pedestrian
prière de... – please do not...
la queue – queue
sens interdit – no entry
sens unique – one-way
la tour – tower
le trottoir – pavement

l'embouteillage

le passage clouté

In town (En ville)

la banlieue – suburbs
la fontaine – fountain
les gens (m/f, pl) – people
l'habitant (m) – inhabitant
l'industrie (f) – industry
le jardin public – park
le parc – park

parisien(ne) – Parisian
le parking – car park
la place – square
le plan – street map
le pont – bridge
le quartier – district

la fontaine

le pont

Buildings (Les bâtiments)

la bibliothèque – library

le bureau des objets trouvés – lost-property office

la cathédrale – cathedral

le centre commercial – shopping centre

le château – castle

le commissariat – police station

l'église (f) – church

la gendarmerie – police station

l'hôpital (m) – hospital

l'hôtel de ville (m) – town hall

la mairie – town hall

l'immeuble (m) – block of flats

le monument – monument

le musée – museum

l'office de tourisme (f) – tourist office

la piscine – swimming pool

l'usine (f) – factory

Conversation: Grades G–D

AQA ✓
OCR ✓
EDEXCEL ✓
WJEC ✓
CCEA ✓

> The only verb forms used here are 'il y a' and 'se trouve'. That is why it is a Grade G–D conversation.

Quels sont les lieux d'intérêt dans ta région?

Il y a des magasins, l'hôtel de ville, une vieille église et le commissariat de police, et un jardin public.

À quelle distance se trouve ta maison de Londres/de la mer?

Ma maison se trouve à cent dix kilomètres de Londres/de la mer.

Il y a combien d'habitants dans ta ville/ton village?

Il y a huit mille habitants.

Qu'est-ce qu'il y a pour les jeunes?

Il y a des clubs, un cinéma et une patinoire.

Conversation: Grades C–A*

AQA ✓
OCR ✓
EDEXCEL ✓
WJEC ✓
CCEA ✓

> 1 Your chance to give an opinion and justify it.

Quel temps fait-il?

Aujourd'hui il pleut.

Quel temps a-t-il fait hier?

Il a fait beau.

Et quel temps fera-t-il demain?

Il fera chaud, je crois.

Décris ta ville/ta région. Tu l'aimes?[1]

J'aime bien ma région parce que près d'ici il y a beaucoup de choses intéressantes. Il y a un canal, une rivière, un joli parc, beaucoup de terrains de sport et un cinéma. Pas loin d'ici il y a des usines mais il y a aussi la campagne.

Où exactement se trouve ta région?

Elle se trouve dans le nord/sud/est/ouest/centre de l'Angleterre/du pays de Galles/de l'Écosse/de l'Irlande.

Quels sont les bâtiments intéressants?

Il y a une bibliothèque, un cinéma, l'hôtel de ville, une vieille église, une piscine et un hôpital.

> 2 Your chance to use a perfect tense.
>
> 3 Your chance to show you can use a future tense (see page 120).

Où es-tu né(e)? Dans cette région?[2]

Non, je suis né(e) à Londres.

Où habiteras-tu à l'avenir?[3]

J'habiterai ici parce que j'aime bien cette région.

5.3 The environment

LEARNING SUMMARY

After studying this section, you should be able to:

- name different endangered species
- describe and give views about dangers to the environment
- talk about how you help the environment

Environmental issues

AQA	✓
OCR	✓
EDEXCEL	✗
WJEC	✓
CCEA	✓

The following vocabulary and sentences will help you in the listening and reading exams, and in the controlled assessment.

Endangered species (Les espèces menacées)

la baleine – whale

la chauve-souris – bat

le dauphin – dolphin

l'éléphant (m) – elephant

le guépard – cheetah

les oiseaux (m) – birds

l'ours (m) – bear

le panda – panda

le phoque – seal

les poissons (m) – fish

le rhinocéros – rhino

le tigre – tiger

> **KEY POINT**
>
> Nearly all **-aux** words (e.g. **les oiseaux**) are masculine but one exception is **la peau** (skin).

Dangers to the environment

On devrait protéger les espèces menacées.
We should protect threatened species.
La baleine est en danger de disparition.
The whale is in danger of disappearing.
La mer polluée tue les poissons.
The polluted sea kills off the fish.
Le réchauffement de la Terre menace les ours blancs.
Global warming threatens polar bears.
Il ne faut pas tuer les baleines.
We should not kill whales.

> **KEY POINT**
>
> **Il faut** and **on devrait** both mean 'we should'.

The local environment

Ma ville est calme/tranquille/bruyante/industrielle.
My city is quiet/quiet/noisy/industrial.
L'air est sale/pollué/propre.
The air is dirty/polluted/clean.

Il y a trop d'usines et de voitures.

There are too many factories and cars.

Les gens laissent tomber des papiers par terre.

People drop litter.

L'air et la rivière deviennent pollués.

The air and the river become polluted.

Devenir means 'to become'.

Il faut un centre de recyclage.

We need a recycling facility.

Les gaz d'échappement polluent l'air.

Exhaust fumes pollute the air.

Les embouteillages aux heures d'affluence polluent l'air.

The traffic jams at rush hour pollute the air.

On n'utilise pas les transports en commun.

People do not use public transport.

Il faut améliorer les transports en commun.

We must improve public transport.

On a créé des zones piétonnes et des pistes cyclables.

They have created pedestrian zones and cycle lanes.

Les voitures sont interdites au centre-ville.

Cars are banned from the city centre.

Il faut payer les sacs en plastique.

You have to pay for plastic bags.

On devrait construire moins de nouvelles routes et d'aéroports.

We should build fewer new roads and airports.

What I do for the environment

Je fais ce que je peux pour protéger l'environnement.

I do what I can to protect the environment.

Je fais du vélo.

I cycle.

Je vais à pied.

I walk.

J'utilise les transports en commun.

I use public transport.

Je ramasse des papiers dans le parc.

I pick up litter in the park.

J'éteins les lumières et je ferme les robinets.

I switch off lights and turn off taps.

J'encourage les gens à ne pas prendre leur voiture.

I encourage people not to use their car.

Je recycle le carton, le papier, les bouteilles. le plastique et les emballages.

I recycle cardboard, paper, bottles, plastic and packaging.

Je réutilise les sacs en plastique.

I re-use plastic bags.

Adjectives

bruyant(e) – noisy
calme – calm
pollué(e) – polluted
propre – clean

sale – dirty
mondial(e) – worldwide
renouvelable – renewable
surpeuplé – overpopulated

Issues (Les problèmes)

le charbon – coal
la consommation – consumption
la couche d'ozone – ozone layer
le déboisement – deforestation
les déchets (m, pl) – waste
les détritus (m, pl) – waste
l'effet (m) de serre – the greenhouse effect
l'énergie (f) éolienne – wind power
l'énergie (f) nucléaire – nuclear energy
l'énergie (f) solaire – solar power

l'essence (f) – petrol
la fumée – smoke
les ordures (f, pl) – rubbish
les papiers (m, pl) – litter
la poubelle – bin
la pluie acide – acid rain
le réchauffement de la Terre – global warming
les ressources (f, pl) – resources
la Terre – Earth

l'effet de serre   la pluie acide   le réchauffement de la Terre

Verbs

améliorer – to improve
augmenter – to increase
conserver – to conserve, to preserve
créer – to create
diminuer – to reduce

disparaître – to disappear
détruire – to destroy
endommager – to damage
gaspiller – to waste
menacer – to threaten
nettoyer – to clean

protéger – to protect
produire – to produce
sauver – to save
supprimer – to get rid of

PROGRESS CHECK

Say or write the following in French:
1. The whale is in danger of disappearing.
2. People drop litter.
3. You have to pay for plastic bags.
4. My city is quiet/noisy/industrial.
5. We should build fewer new roads and airports.

1. La baleine est en danger de disparition.   2. Les gens laissent tomber des papiers par terre.   3. Il faut payer les sacs en plastique.   4. Ma ville est calme (tranquille)/bruyante/industrielle.   5. On devrait construire moins de nouvelles routes et d'aéroports.

5.4 Grammar

After studying this section, you should be able to understand:

- the imperfect tense
- demonstrative adjectives
- possessive adjectives
- the future tense

The imperfect tense

AQA	✓
OCR	✓
EDEXCEL	✓
WJEC	✓
CCEA	✓

KEY POINT

You use the imperfect when you are saying what you were doing or what you used to do. The imperfect endings are: **-ais**, **-ais**, **-ait**, **-ait**, **-ions**, **-iez**, **-aient**, **-aient**.

To find the stem, use the **nous** part of the present tense without the **-ons**, e.g.:

nous finissons = we finish
The stem is **finiss-**
je finissais = I was finishing

donner

finir	donner
je finissais (I was finishing)	**je donnais** (I was giving)
tu finissais (you (singular) were finishing)	**tu donnais** (you (singular) were giving)
il finissait (he was finishing)	**il donnait** (he was giving)
elle finissait (she was finishing)	**elle donnait** (she was giving)
nous finissions (we were finishing)	**nous donnions** (we were giving)
vous finissiez (you (pl) were finishing)	**vous donniez** (you (pl) were giving)
ils finissaient (they (m) were finishing)	**ils donnaient** (they (m) were giving)
elles finissaient (they (f) were finishing)	**elles donnaient** (they (f) were giving)

The only exception is **être**.

être	
j'étais (I was)	**nous étions** (we were)
tu étais (you (singular) were)	**vous étiez** (you (plural) were)
il était (he was)	**ils étaient** (they (m) were)
elle était (she was)	**elles étaient** (they (f) were)

J'allais voir ma tante le dimanche.
I used to go and see my aunt on Sundays.
Je descendais la rue quand je l'ai vu.
I was walking down the road when I saw him.

KEY POINT

If you want to pick up some marks in your speaking and writing, learn two or three imperfects off by heart and include them in your work, e.g. **il pleuvait** (it was raining), **je portais mon pull neuf** (I was wearing my new sweater).

Complete the blanks by adding the correct imperfect ending to each word.

1. Je regard............. la télé quand j'ai entendu le bruit.
   I was watching TV when I heard the noise.

2. Il all............. au cinéma avec moi.
   He used to go to the cinema with me.

Demonstrative adjectives (this, that, these, those)

AQA	✓
OCR	✓
EDEXCEL	✓
WJEC	✓
CCEA	✓

There are four forms of demonstrative adjectives in French.

ce journal   this paper, that paper (masculine singular)

cet ami   this friend, that friend (masculine singular beginning with a vowel or silent 'h')

cette table   this table, that table (feminine singular)

ces élèves   these pupils, those pupils (masculine and feminine plural)

Note that the masculine and feminine plurals are not different as you might have expected.

Say or write the following in French:

1. This pencil
2. This window
3. These pencils
4. These windows

Possessive adjectives

AQA	✓
OCR	✓
EDEXCEL	✓
WJEC	✓
CCEA	✓

Possessive adjectives correspond to 'my', 'your', etc. in English.

	masculine sing.	feminine sing.	masc./fem. plural
my	**mon livre**	**ma chaise**	**mes livres**
your	**ton livre**	**ta chaise**	**tes livres**
his/her	**son livre**	**sa chaise**	**ses livres**
our	**notre pays**	**notre famille**	**nos familles**
your	**votre pays**	**votre famille**	**vos familles**
their	**leur pays**	**leur famille**	**leurs familles**

The possessive adjective agrees with the object possessed (e.g. the book, the chair), not the person who owns it.

Say or write the following in French:

1. My dog
2. His dog
3. Her dog
4. Our house
5. Their house
6. Your garden

The future tense

AQA	✓
OCR	✓
EDEXCEL	✓
WJEC	✓
CCEA	✓

Regular futures

> **KEY POINT**
>
> The future endings are added to the whole of the infinitive.

The endings are: **-ai**, **-as**, **-a**, **-a**, **-ons**, **-ez**, **-ont**, **-ont**. These endings come from the present tense of **avoir**.

-er verbs	-ir verbs	-re verbs
donner	finir	vendre
je donnerai (I will give)	**je finirai** (I will finish)	**je vendrai** (I will sell)
tu donneras	**tu finiras**	**tu vendras**
il donnera	**il finira**	**il vendra**
elle donnera	**elle finira**	**elle vendra**
nous donnerons	**nous finirons**	**nous vendrons**
vous donnerez	**vous finirez**	**vous vendrez**
ils donneront	**ils finiront**	**ils vendront**
elles donneront	**elles finiront**	**elles vendront**

> **KEY POINT**
>
> With **-re** verbs, leave the final **-e** off the infinitive.

Irregular futures

aller	**j'irai**	I will go
avoir	**j'aurai**	I will have
devoir	**je devrai**	I will have to
envoyer	**j'enverrai**	I will send
être	**je serai**	I will be
faire	**je ferai**	I will do/make
pouvoir	**je pourrai**	I will be able
recevoir	**je recevrai**	I will receive
savoir	**je saurai**	I will know
venir	**je viendrai**	I will come
voir	**je verrai**	I will see
vouloir	**je voudrai**	I will want

> **PROGRESS CHECK**
>
> Say or write the following in French:
> 1. On Saturday I will play football and I will watch TV.
> 2. This evening I will finish my homework.
> 3. Then I will go out.
> 4. I will see my friends.
> 5. I will be a doctor.
>
> 1. Samedi je jouerai au football et je regarderai la télé.
> 2. Ce soir je finirai mes devoirs.
> 3. Ensuite je sortirai.
> 4. Je verrai mes amis.
> 5. Je serai médecin.

Sample controlled assessment

Speaking

1 TRACK 29 You are going to have a conversation with your teacher about environmental problems. Your teacher will ask about...

- the kind of problems affecting the planet
- your attitude to flooding
- possible solutions.

Teacher: Quels problèmes vois-tu en ce qui concerne l'environnement?

Student: Nous maltraitons la Terre. Quel désastre![9] Chaque année la situation se détériore.[16] Les habitants des pays du nord utilisent énormément[16] d'énergie. Chacun consomme l'équivalent de dix tonnes de charbon par an. L'homme est une espèce menacée. On brûle les forêts qui[30] consomment le CO_2. Au Brésil, on a brûlé des milliers de km^2 en une année. On pollue l'air, on empoisonne nos rivières et nos mers, on traite la planète comme une poubelle, on modifie les plantes et les animaux, on enterre des déchets nucléaires et on détruit les ressources naturelles. La couche d'ozone disparaît à cause des gaz d'échappement. Cela cause l'effet de serre et le réchauffement de la Terre. L'effet de serre, c'est un cercle vicieux.[3] Nous produisons des gaz toxiques qui[30] montent dans l'atmosphère. La chaleur du soleil monte, mais elle est bloquée par les gaz. La Terre devient de plus en plus[16] chaude. Les mers montent et beaucoup d'espèces sont menacées. Notre consommation d'énergie est trop élevée et la planète en[32] souffre.

Teacher: Et les inondations?

Student: La neige fond, la pluie tombe, les rivières débordent, les champs sont inondés, et les rues sont submergées. Les gens sont forcés de quitter leurs maisons, les maisons sont abîmées, le paysage est dévasté et des milliers de gens meurent. Bientôt on n'aura plus[24] de combustibles fossiles.

Teacher: Et la solution?

Student: Les gouvernements ferment les yeux sur le problème. Il faut changer nos habitudes, et il faut qu'on fasse[25] un plan d'action. Il ne nous[32] reste pas[24] beaucoup de temps. Il faut planter des arbres pour remplacer[31] les forêts brûlées. On devrait[14] utiliser les transports en commun pour réduire[31] la pollution. On doit prendre une douche et non pas un bain pour sauvegarder[31] les ressources de la Terre et pour réduire[31] la consommation d'eau. Il faut tout recycler. On doit utiliser des panneaux solaires, installer un double-vitrage et isoler la maison. On doit prendre son vélo pour réduire les émissions de CO_2 et pour diminuer la consommation d'essence. La voiture représente la liberté, mais aussi la pollution. Si on n'utilisait[13] pas la voiture, on consommerait[14] moins d'essence. Si on prenait le bus et le train, on ne polluerait plus l'atmosphère, on respirerait de l'air pur, on pourrait faire plus d'exercice, on serait moins stressé et on se sentirait mieux.

Turn to page 156 for a translation of this passage.

Examiner's comments

This student has delivered a fine performance by demonstrating a good knowledge of grammatical structures (refer to '32 points for improving your grade' on pages 8–10) and by using a wealth of environment-related vocabulary:

3 An extended point of view

9 An exclamation

13 An example of the imperfect

14 Examples of conditionals

16 Impressive vocabulary and structures, e.g. 'énormément', 'de plus en plus'

24 Examples of negatives

25 A subjunctive has been included. Very impressive!

30 'Qui' is a good connective

31 Examples of 'pour' + the infinitive

32 Examples of pronouns

Sample controlled assessment

Writing

1 Write about how you help the environment. You could include...

- why we need to protect the environment
- what you do to help the environment during your daily routine
- what you do to save energy
- your attitude to car travel
- your attitude to recycling
- action you have taken to try to influence other people.

Je fais ce que je peux pour protéger[31] l'environnement. Malgré[19] nos efforts, notre planète est sur le point de[21] mourir. Quel désastre![9]

Je me déplace à pied ou à vélo. Je ne monte jamais[24] dans une voiture. J'ai décidé d'utiliser[4] les transports en commun. Je ne jette rien par terre. Je ramasse même[16] des papiers dans le parc.

Je ne gaspille jamais d'énergie. Avant de sortir,[6] j'éteins les lumières et ferme les robinets. Mes parents ont installé des panneaux solaires et un double-vitrage, et notre maison est vraiment[18] bien isolée. Après avoir pris[8] un bain ou une douche, j'arrose le jardin avec l'eau que j'ai utilisée.[16]

En parlant[7] aux gens, je les encourage à ne pas prendre leur voiture. La voiture représente la liberté mais aussi la pollution. Si on n'utilisait pas la voiture, on consommerait[14] moins d'essence. Si on prenait le bus et le train, on ne polluerait plus l'atmosphère, on respirerait de l'air pur, on pourrait faire plus d'exercice, on serait moins stressé et on se sentirait mieux.[3]

Chez moi il faut absolument qu'on fasse du recyclage.[25] Je recycle le carton, le papier, les bouteilles, le plastique et les emballages. Je réutilise les sacs en plastique. Nous faisons du compost avec les déchets organiques. Je me sers des piles rechargeables pour protéger l'environnement. Quand j'achète par exemple du papier, j'essaie d'en acheter fait à partir des matières recyclées. Je donne les vêtements que je ne porte plus[24] aux œuvres caritatives. Avant d'acheter[6] quelque chose, je me demande si j'en ai vraiment besoin.[1]

J'ai écrit une lettre au premier ministre. Je lui ai dit qu'on doit réduire le volume d'emballage par produit, créer plus de centres de recyclage, créer des pistes cyclables partout dans les grandes villes, planter des arbres le long des rues et améliorer les transports en commun. En plus, je lui ai dit d'interdire les voitures au centre-ville et les sacs en plastique gratuits. On devrait construire moins de nouvelles routes et d'aéroports aussi.

Turn to page 156 for a translation of this passage.

Examiner's comments

This excellent example is about the right length for an A* and it uses a number of the '32 points for improving your grade' from pages 8–10:

1 An 'avoir' structure
3 A justified point of view
4 'J'ai décidé de...'
6 Two examples of 'avant de...'
7 'En' + the present participle
8 'Après avoir' + the past participle
9 An exclamation
14 An example of a conditional
16 Impressive vocabulary. Note that the extra '-e' is due to a preceding direct object in 'l'eau que j'ai utilisée'.
18 'Vraiment' has been used here
19 'Malgré' is used here
21 'Sur le point de'
24 Two examples of a negative
25 A subjunctive has been used
31 'Pour' + the infinitive

Exam practice questions

Listening

1 Where are they going? Which direction? **Tick the correct boxes.**

Section 1

(a) She is going:

A 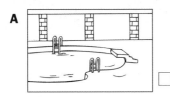 ☐   B  ☐   C  ☐

(b) She must:

A  ☐   B ☐   C ☐

Section 2

(c) He is going:

A  ☐   B  ☐   C  ☐

(d) He must:

A ☐   B ☐   C ☐

Section 3

(e) She is going:

A  ☐   B ☐   C ☐

(f) She must:

A  ☐   B ☐   C ☐

(6)

WJEC Foundation Tier

Exam practice questions

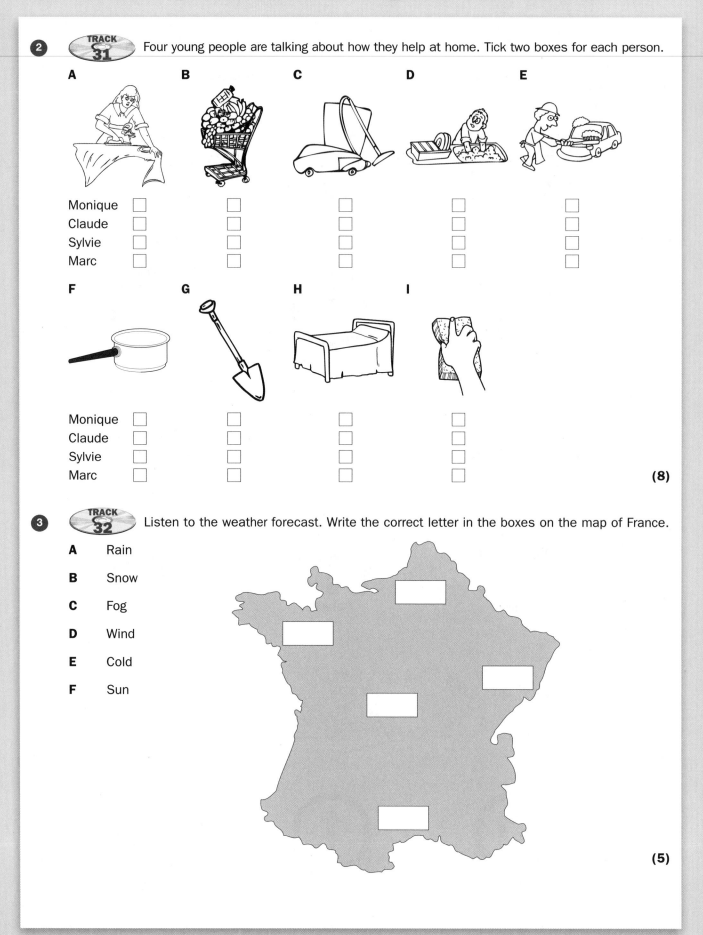

2 **TRACK 31** Four young people are talking about how they help at home. Tick two boxes for each person.

A   B   C   D   E

	A	B	C	D	E
Monique	☐	☐	☐	☐	☐
Claude	☐	☐	☐	☐	☐
Sylvie	☐	☐	☐	☐	☐
Marc	☐	☐	☐	☐	☐

F   G   H   I

	F	G	H	I
Monique	☐	☐	☐	☐
Claude	☐	☐	☐	☐
Sylvie	☐	☐	☐	☐
Marc	☐	☐	☐	☐

(8)

3 **TRACK 32** Listen to the weather forecast. Write the correct letter in the boxes on the map of France.

A   Rain

B   Snow

C   Fog

D   Wind

E   Cold

F   Sun

(5)

Exam practice questions

Reading

1 Read the e-mail message below and look at the plan that follows.

> Bientôt tu seras chez nous. Dans le fichier il y a un petit plan de l'appartement. La cuisine
> est à droite en entrant. En face de la cuisine il y a la salle de bains. La salle de séjour est à
> côté de la salle de bains. A côté de la salle de séjour, à gauche il y a la chambre de grand-mère.
> Ma chambre est au fond du couloir à gauche et en face il y a la chambre de mes parents.
>
> A bientôt
> Céline.
>
> Plan de notre appartement:

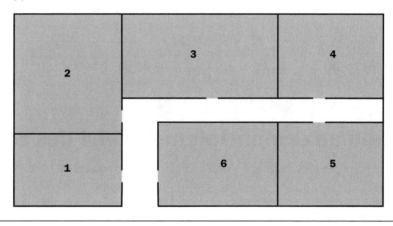

Using the information in the e-mail, match each room to the descriptions given below. Write a number in each answer space.

(a) Céline's bedroom ....

(b) Kitchen ....

(c) Bathroom ....

(d) Grandmother's bedroom ....

(e) Parents' bedroom ....

(f) Living room .... **(6)**

Exam practice questions

2 Read the text message below. Choose from the words given in the box to complete the sentences.

joue	sortes	quartier	plastique	brique	crimes	enfants	carton

J'habite un **(a)** .... pauvre de Montréal.

Dans ma rue il y a toutes **(b)** .... de maisons.

Pour les riches les maisons sont construites en **(c)** ....

Pour les pauvres elles sont construites en **(d)** ....

Notre rue est très dangereuse. Il y a beaucoup de **(e)** ....

J'aime jouer au foot avec les **(f)** .... dans la rue.

Nous fabriquons le ballon avec des morceaux de **(g)** ....

De temps en temps on **(h)** .... avec un cerf-volant. **(8)**

3 Read the leaflet below, then answer the questions that follow.

Attention aux cambrioleurs! Voici des conseils.

- Fermez toutes les portes à clef. N'oubliez pas le garage!
- Quand vous sortez le soir, laissez une lumière allumée.
- Quand vous partez en vacances, donnez le numéro de téléphone de votre hôtel à un voisin. Laissez une clé à un voisin et demandez-lui d'enlever le courrier de la boîte aux lettres.
- Ne laissez pas les clefs de votre voiture près de la porte d'entrée.
- Faites installer une alarme anti-vol.
- Ne laissez pas les inconnus entrer dans la maison.
- Ne gardez pas de sommes d'argent chez vous.
- Cachez vos bijoux.

(a) What does the leaflet try to prevent? .... **(1)**

(b) What part of the house might you forget to lock? .... **(1)**

(c) What should you do when you go out at night? .... **(1)**

(d) When you go on holiday, what two things should you leave with a neighbour?

   (i) ....   **(ii)** .... **(2)**

(e) How can a neighbour help while you are away on holiday?

   .... **(1)**

(f) What must you not leave near the front door? .... **(1)**

(g) What device could be useful? .... **(1)**

(h) Who must not be allowed in the house? .... **(1)**

(i) What must you not keep at home? .... **(1)**

(j) What should you hide? .... **(1)**

Exam practice questions

4   Here is the weather forecast for four parts of France.

Champagne

Le ciel sera couvert toute la journée. Le vent du nord sera sensible et renforcera l'impression de froid. Le thermomètre ne dépassera pas 4 à 6°C.

Paris

Encore beaucoup de nuages et d'averses sur les versants nord. L'après-midi le thermomètre aura du mal à repasser au-dessus de 0°C.

Gard

Les nuages seront présents avec davantage d'éclaircies l'après-midi. Un risque de neige est possible. Les températures monteront jusqu'à 4°C l'après-midi.

Dordogne

Le temps sera bien ensoleillé avec un vent très fort aux environs de 100 à 110km/h. L'après-midi le thermomètre indiquera entre 5 et 10°C.

Answer the following questions.

(a)   Which area will be sunniest? ....

(b)   In which area is it likely to snow? ....

(c)   Where will the temperature struggle to get above freezing? ....

(d)   Where will the wind make it feel even colder than it really is? .... **(4)**

5   Read the letter below, then answer the questions that follow.

L'ENVIRONNEMENT

Protéger l'environnement, c'est la chose la plus importante pour moi mais ce qui m'étonne, c'est que certains jeunes ne font pas attention à leur environnement. Ils se contentent d'éparpiller des papiers partout dans la rue, ou sur les plages. Le nombre de gens qui se déplacent en voiture est inquiétant, malgré le fait que le transport en commun marche très bien. Par exemple, j'essaie de persuader mon père d'utiliser le train au lieu de sa voiture tous les jours, mais cela ne sert à rien - il ne m'écoute pas et dit que voyager en voiture lui convient mieux. Pour le convaincre, évidemment, c'est trop tard.

Mes amis et moi, nous avons fait des efforts récemment pour faire revivre la flore et la faune qui étaient en train de disparaître. Ce type d'opération doit avoir lieu chaque année. Ce qui est positif, c'est qu'on pense à créer des programmes spéciaux à l'école pour informer les jeunes. Alors je m'attends à d'énormes changements pour l'avenir. Mais le gouvernement devrait faire plus pour protéger l'environnement et dans ce but j'ai écrit de nombreuses lettres.

Adèle

(a)   What is the most important thing for Adèle? ....

(b)   What do some young people do? ....

(c)   What does Adèle find worrying? ....

(d)   According to Adèle, what should her father do? ....

(e)   What have Adèle and her friends tried to do? ....

(f)   What has Adèle done to try to convince the government? .... **(6)**

Education and work

The following topics are covered in this chapter:

- **School and college**
- **Pressures and problems at school**
- **Jobs**
- **Grammar**

6.1 School and college

LEARNING SUMMARY

After studying this section, you should be able to:

- describe your school and school routine
- understand information about a school in a French-speaking country
- say what you like and dislike about school, giving reasons

School and college

AQA	✓
OCR	✓
EDEXCEL	✓
WJEC	✓
CCEA	✓

The following vocabulary will help you in the listening and reading exams. Your teacher is likely to ask you to describe your school in the controlled speaking assessment. You should learn answers to all the obvious questions: questions about your subjects, the school building itself, the teachers and your plans for after school. You should realise that you may be tested on your tenses by questions about what you did yesterday at school and what you will do tomorrow. You may also be asked an opinion about your school.

Back to school (La rentrée)

l'examen

le bac(calauréat) – an exam that is the equivalent of A-level
la classe – class
les devoirs (m, pl) – homework
l'échange (m) – exchange
l'emploi du temps (m) – timetable
en sixième – in Year 7
en cinquième – in Year 8
l'épreuve (f) – test
l'erreur (f) – mistake
l'examen (m) – examination
par exemple – for example

la faute – fault, mistake
les grandes vacances (f, pl) – summer holidays
la leçon – lesson
la matière – subject
le mot – word
la pause du midi – lunchtime
la phrase – sentence
la récréation – break
le tableau – board
le trimestre – term

Subjects (Les matières)

l'allemand (m) – German
l'anglais (m) – English
la biologie – biology
la chimie – chemistry
le commerce – commerce, business studies
le dessin – art, drawing
l'éducation physique (f) – physical education
EMT (éducation manuelle et technique) – CDT

EPS (éducation physique et sportive) – PE
l'espagnol (m) – Spanish
le français – French
la géographie – geography
la gymnastique – gymnastics
l'histoire (f) – history
l'informatique (f) – computing, IT
les langues modernes (f, pl) – modern languages

le latin – Latin
les maths (f, pl) – maths
les mathématiques (f, pl) – maths
la physique – physics
la science – science
les sciences naturelles (f, pl) – biology
la technologie – technology
les travaux manuels (m, pl) – handicraft

l'emploi du temps

	Lundi	Mardi	Mercredi	Jeudi	Vendredi
08:15					
	Dessin	Espagnol		Maths	Histoire
09:10					
	Français	Français	Français	Histoire	Français
10:20					
	Français	Maths	Maths	Espagnol	Français
11:15					
	Maths		Histoire	Anglais	Maths
12:10					
13:45					
	Espagnol	Technologie		Anglais	EPS
14:40					
	Technologie	Physique		Anglais	EPS
15:35					
	Musique	Espagnol		Physique	Biologie
16:45					

Adjectives

absent(e) – absent
excellent(e) – excellent
faux (fausse) – false, wrong

juste – correct
mixte – mixed
primaire – primary

privé(e) – private
scolaire – school
secondaire – secondary

At school (À l'école/au collège)

le laboratoire

CES (Collège d'Enseignement Secondaire) – secondary school (up to age 15)
la cantine – canteen
le collège – school (secondary)
le couloir – corridor
la cour – playground
l'école (f) – school (primary)

le gymnase – gym
le laboratoire – laboratory
le lycée – secondary school (ages 15 and over)
la salle de classe – classroom
la salle de musique – music room
la salle des professeurs – staff room
les toilettes – toilets

la salle de classe	la cantine	le gymnase	le laboratoire	la salle de classe
le couloir				
la salle de classe	la salle de classe	la salle de musique	la salle des professeurs	la salle de classe
la salle de classe	la cour			la salle de classe
la salle de classe	la salle de classe	la salle de classe	les toilettes	la salle de classe

Equipment (L'équipement)

le bic – pen

le cahier – exercise book

la calculatrice – calculator

le cartable – school bag

le crayon – pencil

la gomme – rubber

la règle – rule, ruler

le stylo – pen

le stylo à encre – fountain pen

l'uniforme scolaire (m) – school uniform

l'institutrice

MME SMITH

Staff (Les membres du personnel)

le/la concierge – caretaker, janitor

le directeur/la directrice – headmaster/mistress

l'élève (m/f) – pupil

l'enseignant(e) (m/f) – teacher

l'instituteur, -trice (m/f) – teacher (primary school)

le maître – master

le professeur – teacher

le/la secrétaire – secretary

Verbs

apprendre – to learn

bavarder – to chat

cocher – to tick

corriger – to correct

décrire – to describe

écouter – to listen

écrire – to write

s'ennuyer – to be bored

étudier – to study

expliquer – to explain

faire attention – to be careful

frapper – to hit

parler – to talk

punir – to punish

savoir – to know

sonner – to ring

se taire – to stay silent

terminer – to finish

traduire – to translate

PROGRESS CHECK

Say or write the following in French:

1. My favourite subject is chemistry.
2. I am going on an exchange.
3. I hate my school uniform.
4. I learn two languages.
5. I am bored at school.
6. My school is modern and the teachers are nice.
7. Last year, I went on an exchange.

1. Ma matière préférée est la chimie. 2. Je fais un échange. 3. Je déteste mon uniforme scolaire. 4. J'apprends deux langues. 5. Je m'ennuie au collège. 6. Mon collège est moderne et les professeurs sont sympathiques. 7. L'année dernière j'ai fait un échange.

Conversation: Grades G–D

AQA ✓
OCR ✓
EDEXCEL ✓
WJEC ✓
CCEA ✓

Make sure you can answer these questions without thinking. Get someone to ask you the questions so you can practise answering them without using the book.

🗣 **Quelle est ta matière préférée?**
🗣 Je préfère le français.
🗣 **Pourquoi?**
🗣 J'aime bien le professeur.
🗣 **Il y a une matière que tu n'aimes pas?**
🗣 Je n'aime pas les sciences.
🗣 **Tu fais du sport au collège?**
🗣 Je joue au tennis, au football, au hockey.
🗣 **Comment viens-tu au collège?**
🗣 Je viens à pied/en voiture/en car.
🗣 **Comment es-tu venu(e) ce matin?**
🗣 Je suis venu(e) à pied.[1]
🗣 **À quelle heure arrives-tu au collège?**
🗣 J'arrive à neuf heures moins le quart.[2]
🗣 **Les cours commencent à quelle heure?**
🗣 Les cours commencent à neuf heures.
🗣 **Tu as combien de cours par jour?**
🗣 J'en ai cinq.
🗣 **Chaque cours dure combien de temps?**
🗣 Un cours dure une heure.
🗣 **À quelle heure est la récréation?**
🗣 La récréation est à onze heures.
🗣 **Combien de temps dure la récréation?**
🗣 La récréation dure un quart d'heure.
🗣 **Qu'est-ce que tu fais pendant la récréation?**
🗣 Je mange, je bois quelque chose et je cause avec mes amis.[3]

1 You have used a perfect tense!

2 You could also say 'à huit heures quarante-cinq'.

3 The more you say, the more marks you get.

Conversation: Grades C–A*

AQA ✓
OCR ✓
EDEXCEL ✓
WJEC ✓
CCEA ✓

Make sure you can answer these questions without thinking. Get someone to ask you the questions so you can practise answering them without using the book.

🗣 **Comment tu te prépares pour le collège le matin?**
🗣 Je me réveille à sept heures, je me lève à sept heures et quart, je me lave, je m'habille et je prends mon petit déjeuner. Je prépare mes livres et je sors.
🗣 **Décris une journée dans ton collège.**
🗣 J'arrive à neuf heures moins cinq, mon professeur fait l'appel et le premier cours commence à neuf heures. J'ai deux cours puis c'est la récréation.
🗣 **Qu'est-ce que tu fais pendant la récréation?**
🗣 Je parle avec mes amis, je mange et je bois quelque chose.
🗣 **Et après?**
🗣 J'ai encore un cours puis c'est l'heure du déjeuner. Quelquefois je rentre chez moi pour manger, quelquefois je mange un sandwich et quelquefois je mange à la cantine. L'après-midi j'ai encore deux cours puis je rentre pour faire mes devoirs.

Décris ton collège.

Une partie est vieille et l'autre partie est moderne. Nous avons des terrains de sport, des laboratoires et une bibliothèque. C'est dommage, nous n'avons pas de piscine.

Et tes matières?

J'étudie huit matières, l'anglais, les maths, le français, les sciences, la technologie, l'allemand, l'histoire et la géographie.

Depuis quand étudies-tu le français?

J'étudie le français depuis cinq ans.[1]

Qu'est-ce que tu as fait au collège hier?

J'ai appris beaucoup de choses. J'ai assisté à cinq cours, j'ai causé avec mes amis et je suis allé(e) au terrain de sport où j'ai joué au tennis.[2]

Qu'est-ce que tu feras ce soir?[3]

Je ferai mes devoirs et je sortirai avec mes amis.

Tu aimes ton collège?[4]

J'aime bien le collège, j'adore les sports mais je déteste les devoirs.

Pourquoi tu détestes les devoirs?[5]

Parce qu'il y a tant d'autres choses que je voudrais faire.

1. A 'depuis' structure.
2. Show you can use not only the perfect tense with 'avoir', but also the perfect tense with 'être'.
3. Your chance to show you can use the future tense.
4. Your chance to show you can give opinions.
5. Your chance to show you can justify your opinions.

> **KEY POINT**
>
> **Quelquefois** means 'sometimes'.
> **Tant de** means 'so many'.

6.2 Pressures and problems at school

LEARNING SUMMARY

After studying this section, you should be able to:
- describe the pressures and problems of school life
- explain what you must do and should not do at school

Pressures and problems at school

AQA	✓
OCR	✓
EDEXCEL	✓
WJEC	✓
CCEA	✓

The following vocabulary and sentences will help you in the listening and reading exams, and in the controlled assessment.

Pressures (Les pressions)

le baccalauréat (le bac) – an exam that is the equivalent of A-levels

le brevet – an exam taken at the end of college (nearly the equivalent of GCSE)

le bulletin – school report

extra-scolaire – extra-curricular

les notes (f, pl) – marks

le stress – stress

stressant(e)/stressé(e) – stressful/stressed

What is not allowed in school

se maquiller

Il est interdit de/d'... On ne devrait pas... Il ne faut pas...	We are not allowed to...
choisir ce qu'on porte	choose what we wear
se maquiller ou porter des bijoux	put on make-up or wear jewellery
parler quand le prof parle	speak when the teacher is speaking
donner nos opinions	give our opinions
être insolent	be cheeky
manger, boire quelque chose en classe	eat, drink in class
arriver en retard	arrive late
sortir de l'école	leave the school
avoir le chewing-gum	have chewing gum

What we have to do in school

Il faut... On doit...	We have to...
travailler dur	work hard
écouter et respecter nos professeurs	listen to and respect our teachers
porter un uniforme laid	wear an ugly uniform
prêter attention tout le temps	pay attention all the time

Sources of stress

J'en ai marre de l'école.

I am fed up with school.

Je ne suis qu'un nom sur une liste.

I am only a name on a list.

> **KEY POINT**
>
> **Ne ... que** means 'only'.

Le règlement n'est pas raisonnable.

The rules are unfair.

La journée scolaire est très stressante.

The school day is stressful.

J'ai un prof de langues sans autorité, qui ne sait pas préparer ses leçons.

I have a language teacher who has no authority and who cannot prepare his/her lessons.

L'uniforme est affreux. Bien qu'il soit bon pour la discipline, il est laid et peu élegant. Tout le monde se ressemble.

The uniform is awful. Although it is good for discipline, it is ugly and not very elegant. Everybody looks the same.

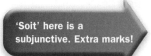

'Soit' here is a subjunctive. Extra marks!

Il y a de la violence et des graffitis.

There is violence and graffiti.

Je rate tout, je ne progresse plus et tous mes résultats sont catastrophiques.

I fail everything, I am no longer making progress and all my results are catastrophic.

> **KEY POINT**
>
> **Ne ... plus** means 'no longer'.

Il faut que j'aie de bonnes notes tout le temps.

I have to get good marks all the time.

Les profs ne nous écoutent pas et ne nous comprennent pas.

The teachers do not listen to us and do not understand us.

Ils nous donnent trop de devoirs.

They give us too much homework.

Pour passer le bac, j'ai besoin de bonnes notes.

To take A-levels, I need good marks.

> **KEY POINT**
>
> **Passer** in the sentence above does not mean 'to pass'. It means 'to take/sit'.

Je déteste toutes mes matières et tous mes profs.

I hate all my subjects and all my teachers.

Les activités extra-scolaires n'existent pas.

There are no extra-curricular activities.

Je ne comprends rien en chimie.

I understand nothing in chemistry.

Le prof n'explique rien.

The teacher does not explain anything.

Quelques élèves font trop de bruit et je n'entends pas le prof.

Some pupils make too much noise and I cannot hear the teacher.

Je n'ai pas le temps de faire tout ce qu'on me demande.

I do not have time to do everything I am supposed to.

Mes parents me mettent sous trop de pression.

My parents put me under too much pressure.

On travaille tout le temps et on n'a pas de temps pour les loisirs.

We work all the time and we do not have time for leisure activities.

Les profs ne s'intéressent pas à moi.

The teachers are not interested in me.

Les terrains de foot sont trop petits.

The football pitches are too small.

On n'a pas assez d'équipement.

We do not have enough equipment.

Je ne m'entends pas très bien avec mes profs.

I do not get on very well with my teachers.

> **KEY POINT**
>
> **Entendre** means 'to hear' but **s'entendre avec** means 'to get on with'.

Dans mon collège, l'ambiance est affreuse.

The atmosphere in my school is awful.

> **PROGRESS CHECK**
>
> Say or write the following in French:
> 1. It is forbidden to smoke.
> 2. The school day is very stressful.
> 3. The uniform is awful.
> 4. They give us too much homework.
> 5. I cannot hear the teacher.
>
> 1. Il est interdit de fumer.
> 2. La journée scolaire est très stressante.
> 3. L'uniforme est affreux.
> 4. Ils nous donnent trop de devoirs.
> 5. Je n'entends pas le prof.

6.3 Jobs

After studying this section, you should be able to:

- talk about current and future jobs
- outline your future plans
- describe the advantages and disadvantages of different jobs

Current and future jobs

AQA	✓
OCR	✓
EDEXCEL	✓
WJEC	✓
CCEA	✓

You might like to talk about jobs and future plans in your controlled assessments. The future tense is going to be important. You should be ready to talk and write about your work experience. In the listening and reading exams, the words for all the different jobs are always coming up. Learn them!

The world of work (Le monde du travail)

l'annonce (f) – advertisement
le boulot – job (colloquial)
le bureau – office
la carrière – career
la compagnie – company
l'emploi (m) – job
l'employé (m)/l'employée (f) – employee
l'employeur (m) – employer
la formation – training
l'interview (m/f) – interview

la licence – degree (university)
le métier – job, trade, occupation
le patron – boss
le/la propriétaire – owner
le salaire – salary
le stage – training course
le tourisme – tourism
le travail – work
l'université (f) – university
l'usine (f) – factory

Jobs (Les métiers)

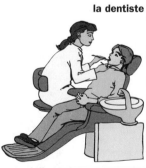
la dentiste

l'agent de police (m) – policeman
l'agriculteur (m) – farmer
l'avocat (m) – lawyer
le caissier/la caissière – cashier
le chauffeur – driver
le chauffeur de taxi – taxi driver
le chef – boss
le chirurgien – surgeon
le coiffeur/la coiffeuse – hairdresser
le commerçant – trader
le comptable – accountant
le/la dentiste – dentist
le docteur – doctor
l'écrivain (m) – writer
le fermier/la fermière – farmer
le gendarme – policeman
l'homme d'affaires (m) – businessman
l'hôtesse de l'air (f) – air hostess
l'infirmier (m)/l'infirmière (f) – nurse

l'informaticien (m)/l'informaticienne (f) – computer operator
l'ingénieur (m) – engineer
le/la journaliste – journalist
le maire – mayor
le marchand – shopkeeper
le marin – sailor
le mécanicien/la mécanicienne – mechanic
le médecin – doctor
la ménagère – housewife
l'ouvrier (m) – manual worker
le pilote – pilot, racing driver
le plombier – plumber
le pompier – fireman
le soldat – soldier
le technicien – technician
le vendeur/la vendeuse – salesperson
le videur/la videuse – bouncer

Verbs and phrases

bâtir – to build

bien payé(e) – well paid

conduire – to drive

employer – to employ, to use

faire un stage – to go on a training course

mal payé(e) – badly paid

poser sa candidature – to apply for a job

quitter – to leave

répondre – to answer

téléphoner – to phone

tomber malade – to fall ill

travailler – to work

Conversation: Grades G–D

AQA	✓
OCR	✓
EDEXCEL	✓
WJEC	✓
CCEA	✓

1 This immediate future tense will earn you marks.

2 Note you do not use the article with 'musicien'.

Qu'est-ce que tu vas faire l'année prochaine?

Je vais continuer mes études. Je vais étudier l'anglais, l'allemand et bien sûr le français.[1]

Et après ton bac, qu'est-ce que tu vas faire?

Je veux aller à l'université pour étudier les langues.

Et après l'université?

Je vais être musicien.[2] Je veux gagner beaucoup d'argent et devenir célèbre.

Conversation: Grades C–A*

AQA	✓
OCR	✓
EDEXCEL	✓
WJEC	✓
CCEA	✓

1 'J'ai travaillé' is an example of the use of the perfect tense.

2 'Je téléphonais' and 'j'écrivais' are examples of the use of the imperfect tense.

3 'Je voyagerai' and 'je travaillerai' are examples of the use of the future tense.

Qu'est-ce que tu as fait comme travail?

Pendant mon stage, j'ai travaillé dans un bureau.[1]

Qu'est-ce que tu as fait exactement?

Je téléphonais aux gens et j'écrivais des lettres.[2]

Le travail te plaisait?

Oui, mais je ne veux pas faire cette sorte de travail à l'avenir.

Qu'est-ce que tu veux faire dans la vie?

Je veux aller à l'université pour étudier la médecine. Après je voyagerai partout dans le monde, puis je travaillerai à Londres.[3] Je veux être médecin.

PROGRESS CHECK

Say or write the following in French:

1 I want to be a doctor.

2 I do not want to work in an office.

3 I worked for a week in a hotel.

4 The work was interesting.

1. Je veux être médecin. 2. Je ne veux pas travailler dans un bureau. 3. J'ai travaillé pendant une semaine dans un hôtel. 4. Le travail était intéressant.

Future plans/advantages and disadvantages of jobs

AQA	✓
OCR	✓
EDEXCEL	✓
WJEC	✓
CCEA	✓

The table below provides some good structures to help you express your views about different jobs.

Je voudrais Je ne voudrais pas Je veux Je ne veux pas J'ai envie de/d' Je n'ai pas envie de/d'	être travailler comme	agent de police dentiste professeur secrétaire vétérinaire (etc.)	parce que car	c'est ce n'est pas	agréable bien payé chouette difficile dur ennuyeux facile fatigant intéressant mal payé monotone satisfaisant stressant varié
	travailler	dehors en plein air à l'intérieur			
		dans	un bureau un magasin une banque une usine une école primaire un collège un hôpital le commerce le marketing le tourisme l'informatique	avec	les enfants les personnes âgées les gens les malades les animaux les ordinateurs

Je voudrais travailler dans un bureau

The following vocabulary and sentences will help you in the listening and reading exams, and in the controlled assessment.

un ordinateur

Describing places of work (Descriptions des lieux de travail)

agréable – pleasant
à l'intérieur – inside
avec – with
c'est... – it is...
ce n'est pas... – it isn't...
chouette – excellent
comme – as
le commerce – business
dehors – outside
difficile – difficult
dur(e) – hard
en plein air – in the open air
les enfants (m/f) – children
ennuyeux (-euse) – boring
être – to be

facile – easy
fatigant(e) – tiring
les gens (m/f, pl) – people
l'informatique (f) – ICT
intéressant(e) – interesting
j'ai envie de... – I want to...
je veux... – I want...
je voudrais... – I would like...
les malades (m/f) – ill people
monotone – monotonous
les ordinateurs (m, pl) – computers
satisfaisant(e) – satisfying
stressant(e) – stressful
varié(e) – varied

KEY POINT

If you find you are using **ennuyeux** (boring) too much, **monotone** (monotonous) is a good alternative.

What I want to do/what I want to be

Je veux devenir journaliste parce que le travail est intéressant et que c'est bien payé.
I want to become a journalist because the work is interesting and it is well paid.
Je vais devenir médecin parce que j'aime aider les gens.
I am going to be a doctor because I like helping people.

KEY POINT

In English, we say 'to want to be a doctor'. The French say 'to want to become a doctor'. **Devenir** means 'to become'.

J'ai décidé que je veux travailler en plein air.
I have decided that I want to work outdoors.
Je suis certain(e) que je ne voudrais pas devenir professeur.
I am sure that I would not like to be a teacher.
Je rêve de devenir footballeur.
I dream of becoming a footballer.
Je vais continuer mes études.
I am going to carry on studying.
J'irai à l'université.
I will go to university.

livrer des journaux

Part-time jobs (Les petits jobs)

aider – to help
commencer – to begin
économiser – to save
faire du babysitting – to babysit
fatigant(e) – tiring
finir – to finish

gagner – to earn
garder des enfants – to babysit
livrer des journaux – to deliver papers
lourd(e) – heavy
recevoir – to receive, to earn
servir – to serve

Part-time work

J'ai un petit job.
I have a part-time job.
Je cherche un petit job.
I am looking for a part-time job.
J'avais un petit job. Je servais les clients.
I used to have a part-time job. I used to serve the customers.

> **KEY POINT**
>
> Notice the use of the imperfect tense above – **j'avais** and **je servais**.

J'ai besoin d'argent.
I need money.
Le week-end, je travaille dans un magasin. Je commence à huit heures et je finis à cinq heures. Je sers les clients.
At weekends, I work in a shop. I start at eight and finish at five. I serve the customers.
Je fais du babysitting pour ma sœur. Je reçois quinze livres.
I babysit for my sister. I get £15.
Je livre des journaux. Je n'aime pas me lever si tôt. Le travail est mal payé. J'arrive au collège fatigué(e). Je gagne six livres de l'heure. Je n'aime pas les jours de pluie. Je ne le fais plus. Je veux gagner de l'argent pour acheter du maquillage et des CD.
I deliver newspapers. I do not like getting up so early. The work is badly paid. I am tired when I get to school. I earn £6 an hour. I do not like the rainy days. I am not doing it anymore. I want to earn money to buy make-up and CDs.
Je veux économiser mon argent pour pouvoir partir en vacances. Mes parents me donnent un peu d'argent. Ils me donnent vingt livres par semaine. Je dois laver la voiture. Ce n'est pas suffisant.
I want to save my money to go on holiday. My parents give me some money. They give me £20 a week.
I have to wash the car. It is not enough.

Work experience

Un stage en entreprise/un stage pratique

Work experience

Au mois d'octobre, j'ai fait un stage pratique sans rémunération.

In October, I did work experience without pay.

Il fallait se lever horriblement tôt.

I had to get up dreadfully early.

J'ai travaillé dans un bureau.

I worked in an office.

J'a commencé à huit heures.

I started at eight.

J'ai fini à cinq heures.

I finished at five.

J'y suis allé(e) en bus.

I travelled there by bus.

J'ai aidé le patron.

I helped the boss.

J'ai appelé les clients.

I phoned the customers.

J'ai répondu au téléphone.

I answered the phone.

J'avais un ordinateur.

I had a computer.

J'ai fait le thé.

I made the tea.

J'ai photocopié des documents.

I photocopied documents.

J'ai servi les clients.

I served the customers.

Chez un vétérinaire

At a vet's

Chez un notaire

At a solicitor's

> **KEY POINT**
>
> **Chez** means 'at the home of' but with a shop or business it means 'at'.

Dans une école/une banque/un magasin/une boulangerie

In a school/bank/shop/bakery

Mon stage était intéressant/ennuyeux/utile/inutile.

My work experience was interesting/boring/useful/useless.

Les gens étaient sympa/méchants.

The people were nice/nasty.

> **PROGRESS CHECK**
>
> Say or write the following in French:
>
> 1 I want to work as a secretary.
> 2 I do not want to work outside.
> 3 My work experience was useful.
> 4 I want to be a journalist.
>
> 1. Je veux travailler comme secrétaire. 2. Je ne veux pas travailler dehors.
> 3. Mon stage était utile. 4. Je veux devenir journaliste.

6.4 Grammar

After studying this section, you should be able to understand:

- the conditional tense
- direct object pronouns
- the pluperfect tense
- negatives

The conditional tense

AQA	✓
OCR	✓
EDEXCEL	✓
WJEC	✓
CCEA	✓

Regular conditionals

> **KEY POINT**
>
> These are the same endings as the imperfect tense. With the conditional, you add the endings to the infinitive. With the imperfect you add them to the stem.

The endings are: **-ais**, **-ais**, **-ait**, **-ait**, **-ions**, **-iez**, **-aient**, **-aient**.

-er verbs
The endings are added to the whole of the infinitive.
donner
je donnerais (I would give)   **nous donnerions** (we would give) **tu donnerais** (you would give)   **vous donneriez** (you (pl) would give) **il donnerait** (he would give)   **ils donneraient** (they (m) would give) **elle donnerait** (she would give)   **elles donneraient** (they (f) would give)
-ir verbs
The endings are added to the whole of the infinitive.
finir
je finirais (I would finish)   **nous finirions** (we would finish) **tu finirais** (you would finish)   **vous finiriez** (you (pl) would finish) **il finirait** (he would finish)   **ils finiraient** (they (m) would finish) **elle finirait** (she would finish)   **elles finiraient** (they (f) would finish)
-re verbs
Leave off the final **-e** of the infinitive.
vendre
je vendrais (I would sell)   **nous vendrions** (we would sell) **tu vendrais** (you would sell)   **vous vendriez** (you (pl) would sell) **il vendrait** (he would sell)   **ils vendraient** (they (m) would sell) **elle vendrait** (she would sell)   **elles vendraient** (they (f) would sell)

Irregular conditionals

> **KEY POINT**
>
> Those verbs that are irregular in the future tense are also irregular in the conditional.

aller	j'irais	I would go
avoir	j'aurais	I would have
devoir	je devrais	I would have to
envoyer	j'enverrais	I would send
être	je serais	I would be
faire	je ferais	I would do/make
pouvoir	je pourrais	I would be able
recevoir	je recevrais	I would receive
savoir	je saurais	I would know
venir	je viendrais	I would come
voir	je verrais	I would see
vouloir	je voudrais	I would want, I would like

> **KEY POINT**
>
> You will get extra marks if you use conditionals in your controlled speaking and writing assessments. The easiest conditional to use is **Je voudrais** (I would like).
>
> **Je voudrais aller en France cet été.**
> I would like to go to France in the summer.
> **Si j'avais de l'argent, j'irais en France.**
> If I had some money, I would go to France.

> **PROGRESS CHECK**
>
> Say or write the following in French:
> 1. I would like to work in an office.
> 2. If I had some money, I would live in the USA.
> 3. That would be great.
> 4. If I was richer, I would go abroad.
>
> 1. Je voudrais travailler dans un bureau. 2. Si j'avais de l'argent, j'habiterais aux États-Unis. 3. Cela serait formidable. 4. Si j'étais plus riche, j'irais à l'étranger.

Direct object pronouns

AQA	✓
OCR	✓
EDEXCEL	✓
WJEC	✓
CCEA	✓

Look at these examples.

He sees me.	**Il me voit.**	He sees us.	**Il nous voit.**
He sees you (sing.).	**Il te voit.**	He sees you (pl.).	**Il vous voit.**
He sees him.	**Il le voit.**	He sees them.	**Il les voit.**
He sees her.	**Il la voit.**		

> **KEY POINT**
>
> There are extra marks available if you can use one of these pronouns in your controlled assessments:
>
> **J'ai beaucoup d'amis et je les vois souvent – surtout le week-end.**
> I have lots of friends and I see them often – especially at the weekend.
> **Mon professeur de français nous aide quand nous avons des problèmes.**
> My French teacher helps us when we have problems.

> **PROGRESS CHECK**
>
> Say or write the following in French:
> ① Peter and Anne? I see him on Fridays and I see her on Saturdays.
>
> 1. Peter et Anne? Je le vois le vendredi et je la vois le samedi.

The pluperfect tense

AQA	✓
OCR	✓
EDEXCEL	✓
WJEC	✓
CCEA	✓

The pluperfect tense is used to say that something had happened, e.g. I had seen…, he had learned…

> **KEY POINT**
>
> In the perfect tense, some verbs use **avoir** and some verbs use **être**. In the pluperfect tense, the same applies. Those verbs that take **être** in the perfect also take **être** in the pluperfect.

To form the pluperfect, use the imperfect tense of **avoir** or **être** and the past participle.

The pluperfect tense with **avoir**:	The pluperfect tense with **être**:
j'avais donné (I had given)	**j'étais allé(e)** (I had gone)
tu avais donné	**tu étais allé(e)**
il/elle/on avait donné	**il/elle/on était allé(e)**
nous avions donné	**nous étions allé(e)s**
vous aviez donné	**vous étiez allé(e)(s)**
ils/elles avaient donné	**ils/elles étaient allé(e)s**

> **KEY POINT**
>
> If you use a pluperfect in your controlled assessment, you will get extra marks. Why not learn a few examples and include them in your work?

Nous avons passé les vacances dans un camping en France. Mon père avait réservé un bon emplacement.
We spent the holidays at a campsite in France. My father had booked a good pitch.
Le jour de mon anniversaire, j'ai reçu l'argent que mes parents m'avaient promis.
On my birthday, I received the money that my parents had promised me.

Say or write the following in French:
1. I had seen the film already.
2. He was late because he had lost the address.

1. J'avais déjà vu le film. 2. Il était en retard parce qu'il avait perdu l'adresse.

Negatives

AQA ✓
OCR ✓
EDEXCEL ✓
WJEC ✓
CCEA ✓

ne ... pas	not
ne ... jamais	never
ne ... personne	nobody/no one
ne ... ni ... (ni ...)	neither ... nor
ne ... plus	no more, no longer
ne ... rien	nothing

Il n'est pas venu.	He did not come.
Il ne paie jamais.	He never pays.
Je ne vois personne.	I see nobody/I cannot see anyone.
Elle n'est ni riche ni pauvre.	She is neither rich nor poor.
Je n'habite plus à Londres.	I do not live in London anymore.
Elle ne mange rien.	She eats nothing.

Try to use negatives in your controlled assessment.

Le jour de mon anniversaire, je n'ai pas reçu l'argent que mes parents m'avaient promis.
On my birthday, I did not receive the money that my parents had promised me.
J'aime le tennis mais je ne joue jamais au football.
I like tennis but I never play football.

Say or write the following in French:
1. I never go to the cinema.
2. At the party, I drank nothing.

1. Je ne vais jamais au cinéma. 2. Pendant la boum, je n'ai rien bu.

Sample controlled assessment

Speaking

1 You are going to have a conversation with your teacher about your plans for the future. Your teacher will ask you to discuss…

- your plans for the future
- your plans for future study
- your reaction to work experience
- marriage.

Teacher: Et tes plans pour l'avenir?

Student: Je viens de[20] faire un stage en entreprise et l'expérience m'a[32] donné des idées pour l'avenir. Il fallait se lever horriblement tôt[16] et je travaillais[13] dans un bureau. Je devais photocopier des documents, répondre au téléphone, appeler les clients et faire le thé. En raison de cette expérience malheureuse,[16] j'ai décidé[4] que je ne veux jamais[24] travailler dans un bureau.

Teacher: Pourquoi?

Student: Parce que[2] le travail était ennuyeux. Plusieurs fois, j'étais sur le point de[21] partir; le travail était tellement[18] monotone. Malgré le fait[19] que mes collègues étaient sympa, j'en avais marre.[1] Ce n'était pas la sorte de travail qu'on m'avait promis.[17] Le patron m'a dit qu'il fallait que je fasse le thé[25] pour les autres. Quelle perte de temps![9] C'était une expérience inoubliable.[15] Heureusement,[16] j'ai appris ce que j'ai envie de[1] faire et ce que je n'ai pas envie de faire.

Teacher: Alors?

Student: Pour commencer,[31] je vais continuer[12] mes études parce que[2] j'ai vu que les gens sans qualifications avaient les pires choses[23] à faire. Ensuite, j'irai à l'université pour obtenir[31] les diplômes nécessaires pour travailler dans une profession libérale. J'ai décidé que je ne veux pas travailler tout le temps en plein air et que je ne veux pas travailler dans un bureau non plus.[24] Je suis certain(e) que je ne voudrais pas[14] devenir professeur. Il est vrai que je rêvais de devenir vedette, mais je crois que je veux devenir journaliste car[30] le travail est intéressant, c'est bien payé et je travaillerais[14] dehors et dedans.

Teacher: Et le mariage?

Student: Je ne me marierai[12] pas[24] avant l'âge de 30 ans et j'aurai[12] trois enfants. Quand j'aurai terminé mes études, j'espère trouver un bon partenaire/une bonne partenaire. Je serai[12] content(e) car[30] je mènerai[12] ma vie de la façon que j'ai choisie. J'habiterai[12] une maison de luxe et je continuerai[12] de travailler pendant que mon/ma partenaire restera à la maison.

Teacher: Le mariage est-il important pour toi?

Student: Le mariage est important pour les rapports entre le couple. C'est un lien qui unit le couple. Je vais me marier parce qu'il[2] est important pour les enfants d'avoir de la stabilité.

Turn to page 156 for a translation of this passage.

Examiner's comments

This student has boosted his/her grade by using plenty of the '32 points for improving your grade' from pages 8–10:

1 Nice 'avoir' structures

2 Uses of 'parce que'

4 A 'j'ai décidé' structure

9 An exclamation

12 Several future tenses have been used

13 An example of an imperfect

14 Conditionals are used here

15 An example here of an adjective

16 Good vocabulary and structures, e.g. 'horriblement tôt', 'expérience malheureuse', 'heureusement'

17 An example of the pluperfect

18 'Tellement' used instead of 'très'

19 A 'malgré' structure

20 A 'venir de' structure

21 'Sur le point de'

23 An example of a superlative

24 Examples of negatives

25 A subjunctive has been used. Very impressive!

30 'Car' is a good connecting word

31 Examples of 'pour' + the infinitive

32 A pronoun

Sample controlled assessment

Writing

1 Write about the pressures of school life. You could include...

- your attitude to school
- things you like or dislike about school
- your attitude to your teachers
- the contribution of your parents
- a possible solution to your problems.

J'en ai marre[1] de l'école. Je ne reçois pas l'éducation qu'on m'avait promise.[17] Je suis étudiant(e) ici depuis[26] quatre ans. Je trouve que la journée scolaire est très stressante et je suis sur le point d'en[21] devenir malade. Je ne suis qu'un[24] nom sur une liste et le règlement n'est pas raisonnable. Il est interdit de se maquiller et de porter des bijoux, donner notre opinion, fumer, manger, boire quelque chose en classe etc, etc. En se levant,[7] il faut mettre un uniforme laid et affreux. Bien qu'il soit bon[25] pour la discipline, il est laid et peu élégant. Tout le monde se ressemble. C'est le pire collège[23] de la région.

L'ambiance dans mon collège est affreuse. Il y a de la violence et des graffitis. Les activités extra-scolaires n'existent pas. Quelques élèves font trop de bruit et je n'entends pas le prof. Les terrains de foot sont trop petits et on n'a pas assez d'équipement. Quel désastre![9]

Je ne m'entends pas très bien avec mes profs parce qu'ils[2] ne s'intéressent pas à moi.[3] Ils n'expliquent rien,[24] ils ne nous écoutent pas et ne nous comprennent pas. Ils nous donnent trop de devoirs. J'ai un prof de langues sans autorité qui[30] ne sait pas préparer ses leçons. Je n'y comprends rien.[24]

Malgré le fait que[19] je n'ai pas le temps de faire tout ce qu'on me[32] demande, mes parents me mettent sous pression sans réfléchir.[5] On travaille tout le temps et on n'a pas de temps pour les loisirs. Il faut que j'aie[25] de bonnes notes tout le temps. Je rate tout, je ne progresse plus[24] et tous mes résultats sont catastrophiques. J'ai décidé de[4] passer le bac mais pour le faire,[31] malheureusement[16] j'ai besoin de[1] bonnes notes. J'aimerais[14] être étudiant(e) dans un autre collège et je viens de[20] demander à mes parents si je peux changer de collège.

Turn to page 156 for a translation of this passage.

Examiner's comments

This student has improved his/her chances of a top grade by using many of the 32 points outlined on pages 8–10:

1 'Avoir' structures
2 A 'parce que' structure
3 A justified point of view
4 'J'ai décidé de...'
5 'Sans' + the infinitive
7 'En' + the present participle
9 An exclamation
14 An example of a conditional
16 Impressive vocabulary
17 An example of the pluperfect
19 A 'malgré' structure
20 'Venir de'
21 A 'sur le point de' structure
23 An example of a superlative
24 Negatives have been used
25 Extra marks for using subjunctives
26 A 'depuis' structure
30 'Qui' is a good connective
31 'Pour' + the infinitive
32 An example of a pronoun

Exam practice questions

Listening

1 TRACK 34 Marc and Monique are discussing a new teacher.

(a) What is Monique's attitude to the teacher? ....

Give four reasons to justify your answer.

(i) ....

(ii) ....

(iii) ....

(iv) .... **(5)**

(b) What is Marc's attitude to the teacher? ....

Give four reasons to justify your answer.

(i) ....

(ii) ....

(iii) ....

(iv) .... **(5)**

(c) What does Monique say happened that morning?

.... **(1)**

(d) According to Monique, how was the teacher during the lesson?

.... **(2)**

(e) What does Marc say at the end of the conversation?

.... **(1)**

2 TRACK 35 You are in Brittany on holiday. You tune into a local radio station and hear a report.

(a) Why did Alexandre stop going to school?

....

(b) What does Alexandre do to earn money?

....

(c) What does he hope to do with this money?

....

(d) Why do so few children go to school?

.... **(4)**

Exam practice questions

3 **TRACK 36** Listen to the two interviews and complete the grid.

	Interview 1	Interview 2	
Surname	**(a)**	**(e)**	
First name	Sophie	Paul	
Age	**(b)**	**(f)**	
Favourite subject	**(c)**	**(g)**	
Ideal job	**(d)**	**(h)**	**(8)**

4 **TRACK 37** You want to work in France and you hear this radio advert. Answer in English.

(a) Type of work: ....

(b) You must not have: ....

(c) You must speak: ....

(d) Start date: ....

(e) End date: ....

(f) Hours per day: ....

(g) Cost of accommodation: ....

(h) Pay (per week): .... **(8)**

5 **TRACK 38** You are working in an office and you take a phone call. Tick the correct boxes.

(a) Who is phoning?

    A Mr Ferrier ☐   **B** Mrs Ferrier ☐   **C** The boss ☐

(b) Where does Mrs Ferrier work?

    A Abroad ☐   **B** In the foreign department ☐   **C** At a doctor's ☐

(c) What is the problem?

    A A breakdown ☐   **B** A complaint ☐   **C** An illness ☐

(d) Who is with Mrs Ferrier now?

    A The boss ☐   **B** The doctor ☐   **C** A stranger ☐

(e) Where will Mrs Ferrier be tomorrow?

    A At work ☐   **B** At home ☐   **C** Abroad ☐   **(5)**

Exam practice questions

6 **TRACK 39** Listen to this conversation between Luc and his boss, then answer the following questions.

(a) How often has Luc been late? Tick the correct box.

A Never ☐

B Once ☐

C More than once ☐

(b) Why did Luc stay so long at his grandmother's? ....

(c) How did he solve the problem with the breakdown? ....

(d) What caused the traffic jam? ....

(e) What is the boss's attitude to Luc? Tick the correct box.

A He is amused ☐

B He is patient ☐

C He is impatient ☐ **(5)**

7 **TRACK 40** Jean-Pierre is talking about his life near Paris. Are the following statements **true** or **false**? Tick the correct box in each case.

		True	False
(a)	It is easy to find work in the village.	☐	☐
(b)	He would like to work on a farm.	☐	☐
(c)	There are few machines on farms.	☐	☐
(d)	He found work in autumn.	☐	☐
(e)	He works in the fields.	☐	☐
(f)	He works with fruit.	☐	☐
(g)	He wants to work in Paris.	☐	☐
(h)	He knows a lot of people in Paris.	☐	☐
(i)	Traffic is a problem in the village.	☐	☐
(j)	The shops in the village sell everything.	☐	☐

(10)

Exam practice questions

Reading

1 You are about to start work in France. Read the information below and answer the questions that follow.

> - Jours de congé: jeudi et dimanche
> - Vacances: le mois d'août
> - Transport au bureau: prenez l'autobus 79 devant la mairie. Descendez après 4 arrêts.
> - La cantine se trouve au rez-de-chaussée.
> - Interdit de fumer sauf dans le parking.
> - Vêtements: Hommes: Il faut porter une cravate.
>   Femmes: Défense de porter des bijoux.

(a) What are your two days off? ....

(b) When is your holiday period? ....

(c) From where do you take the bus? ....

(d) When do you get off the bus? ....

(e) Where is the canteen? ....

(f) What must men wear? ....

(g) What must women not wear? .... **(7)**

2 Read the following magazine extract and answer the questions that follow.

> ## Videuse de boîte: profession dangereuse
>
> Pauline est videuse de boîte dans un quartier dangereux de Marseille. Pourquoi a-t-elle choisi ce métier dangereux?
>
> Elles en sont actuellement une cinquantaine dans la ville contre deux milles hommes. Mais Pauline est la plus jeune et la plus petite avec son 1,60m. Elle est sans conteste l'une des plus courageuses et elle dit que l'utilisation de son portable améliore les conditions de son travail. L'esprit de solidarité avec les videurs est toujours présent.
>
> A vingt-deux ans, Pauline, jusqu'à récemment mère célibataire d'une petite fille de neuf mois, Sheila, travaille de huit heures du soir à cinq heures du matin. Lors de son divorce, son métier l'a empêchée d'obtenir la garde de son premier enfant, Josef, qui vit avec son père en Belgique.
>
> Pauline maintenant a refait sa vie avec un jeune anglais, Jack, qui est homme au foyer. C'est lui qui garde Sheila.
>
> – Pauline, pourquoi ce métier?
>
> – Un homme ne peut pas fouiller une femme et plein de femmes cachent des drogues sous leurs vêtements. C'est un travail bien payé et dans ce métier le chômage est inconnu!

(a) What is Pauline's job? .... **(1)**

(b) Where exactly is her place of work? .... **(1)**

(c) How many women do this job in Marseille? .... **(1)**

(d) How many men do this job in Marseille? .... **(1)**

(e) How does Pauline stand out from the other women doing this job? Give three reasons.

    (i) ....

    (ii) ....

    (iii) .... **(3)**

Exam practice questions

(f) What device helps Pauline? .... **(1)**

(g) What else helps her in her job? .... **(1)**

(h) What has Pauline been until recently? .... **(1)**

(i) Why was she not given custody of Josef? .... **(1)**

(j) What is Jack's job? .... **(1)**

(k) What can a man not do in this job? .... **(1)**

(l) What is unknown in this job? .... **(1)**

3 Read this e-mail, then answer the questions that follow.

> Michelle,
>
> Je vais décrire le travail que j'ai fait pendant les vacances. J'ai travaillé dans un hôtel près de chez moi. J'ai dû faire les lits, passer l'aspirateur, faire de la cuisine et servir dans le bar. Le travail était intéressant mais fatigant. Je travaillais de huit heures du matin à cinq heures du soir avec une heure à midi pour manger.
>
> J'ai gagné six livres par heure et j'ai reçu des pourboires. L'année prochaine je vais faire le même travail dans le même hôtel. Tu veux y aller avec moi?
>
> A bientôt
> Monique

(a) What four tasks did Monique have to do in the hotel?

   (i) ....

   (ii) ....

   (iii) ....

   (iv) .... **(4)**

(b) What is her opinion of the work? .... **(2)**

(c) How long was the lunch break? .... **(1)**

(d) How much did Monique earn? .... **(1)**

(e) What supplemented her earnings? .... **(1)**

(f) What is Monique going to do next year? .... **(1)**

(g) What does she ask Michelle? .... **(1)**

Exam practice answers

CHAPTER 1

Listening Task 1

(a) B; (b) C; (c) A; (d) B; (e) It will help to keep him in a good physical condition; (f) A; (g) C; (h) C; (i) B

Listening Task 2

(a) C and G; (b) B and H; (c) D and E

Listening Task 3

(a) B; (b) A; (c) C; (d) C; (e) B; (f) C; (g) A; (h) B

Listening Task 4

(a) A; (b) B; (c) B; (d) A; (e) B; (f) A

Reading Task 1

(a) Rose; (b) Luc; (c) Edgar; (d) Claude; (e) Bernadette; (f) Marie; (g) Anne; (h) Jean-Paul; (i) Estelle; (j) Monique; (k) Pierre

Reading Task 2

(a) Monique; (b) Anne; (c) Pierre; (d) Jacques; (e) Monique; (f) Monique; (g) Anne; (h) Monique; (i) Monique

Reading Task 3

(a) A; (b) A; (c) Cod; (d) Prawns; (e) Oysters; (f) C; (g) C; (h) Book; (i) B

Reading Task 4

(a) To the ice rink

(b) She has a sore throat

(c) Flu

(d) She will stay in bed.

(e) Lozenges for the throat.

(f) To the doctor's

(g) Asking Pierre if he wants to go.

Reading Task 5

(a) A; (b) B; (c) A; (d) B; (e) A; (f) C; (g) (i)–(iii) **In any order:** go out; sunbathe; bathe in the pool

Reading Task 6

(a) médicaments; (b) couchez; (c) devant; (d) s'arrêter; (e) peu; (f) cigarettes; (g) causer; (h) fermées; (i) faites

Reading Task 7

(a) Health

(b) He runs 5km a day.

(c) A private detective who is after a serial killer.

(d) Oregon

(e) Road haulage

(f) She is a nurse.

(g) Religious principles

(h) Self-confidence

(i) Journalism

(j) Cooking

(k) (i)–(iv) **In any order:** walking his dogs; playing the violin; listening to music; setting off into nature with his car.

Reading Task 8

(a) (i)–(ii) **In any order:** plays hockey; goes for long walks with the dog.

(b) Slim

(c) Two difficult little sisters

(d) He is a farmer.

(e) On the ground floor

(f) Sharing a bedroom

(g) They always want to watch the other TV channel.

(h) His room

(i) (i)–(ii) **In any order:** smoke; drink alcohol

Reading Task 9

(a) 75 minutes

(b) Croissants and jam

(c) Hot chocolate

(d) By coach/bus

(e) It was in the sales.

(f) It was raining.

(g) She didn't like it.

(h) They avoided traffic jams.

CHAPTER 2

Listening Task 1

(a) 10

(b) is noisy; her bedroom

(c) bicycle

(d) almost an adult

(e) go into town; buy her own clothes

(f) go on holiday with her girlfriends

Listening Task 2

(a) Happy

(b) They are very close.

(c) An acting course

(d) She got lost (in Paris).

(e) She enjoyed fantasies as a child.

(f) She doesn't like it.

Listening Task 3

(a) B

(b) That what she says is stupid

(c) That it is ridiculous

(d) That they are lazy and deserve nothing

(e) C

(f) Poverty

(g) They are happier.

(h) She is hopeful

(i) A

(j) Cry

Reading Task 1

(a) (i) Talk to her parents three days before (ii) They could change their mind.

(b) His friends

(c) Do something to deserve it

(d) Arguing

(e) At weekends

(f) Let his parents know if he is coming home after midnight

(g) Not to be drunk

(h) Sleep all day

(i) She can go out two weekends a month.

(j) (i)–(iii) **In any order:** concerts; night clubs; parties.

(k) Say what time she will be home

(l) She does

(m) Make choices

Reading Task 2

(a) taille; **(b)** blonds; **(c)** aimons; **(d)** oiseaux; **(e)** chômage

Reading Task 3

(a) B; **(b)** C; **(c)** B; **(d)** A; **(e)** C; **(f)** B; **(g)** B

CHAPTER 3

Listening Task 1

cinema; maison; 19; voiture; tard

Listening Task 2

Numéro de téléphone: 03 22 38 56 24

Message: malade; soir; après-demain; cadeau; restaurant; payer

Listening Task 3

(a) Crime

(b) Sport

(c) Bad weather

(d) A politician's visit

(e) Road traffic

Listening Task 4

Marc: C, G and I

Juliette: D, F and H

Listening Task 5

(a) American

(b) Tuesday

(c) 20.00

(d) 7 euros

(e) 03 23 95 67 44

Listening Task 6

(a) A; **(b)** B; **(c)** C

Listening Task 7

(a) Opposite the town hall

(b) Belgian

(c) 15 euros

(d) a drink

(e) service

(f) steak and chips

(g) Tuesdays

Listening Task 8

7.30 – F; 8.00 – G; 8.30 – D; 9.00 – E; 10.00 – C; 11.00 – H; 11.30 – A; 12.00 – B

Reading Task 1

B; D; E; G; H; I

Reading Task 2

(a) Advertisements

(b) They made him repeat his lines.

(c) A year

(d) The protection of wild animals.

(e) Going to fashion houses

(f) Being photographed

(g) They phone the newspapers

(h) Something to do with biology or the environment.

Reading Task 3

(a) 22.30; **(b)** 23.00; **(c)** 19.30; **(d)** 19.00; **(e)** 18.30

Reading Task 4

(a) Edgar; **(b)** Françoise; **(c)** Jacques; **(d)** Pierre; **(e)** Luc; **(f)** Jacqueline; **(g)** Pauline

CHAPTER 4

Listening Task 1

(a) (i) Three; **(ii)** 7pm; **(b)** B and D

Listening Task 2

(a) Wednesdays

(b) 2pm

(c) At the entrance

(d) 1 hour 30 mins

Listening Task 3

(a) Unfavourable

(b) Favourable

(c) Favourable

(d) Unfavourable

(e) Unfavourable

(f) Favourable

Listening Task 4

(a) A; **(b)** D; **(c)** C; **(d)** A; **(e)** D

Listening Task 5

(a) a forest; **(b)** D; **(c)** A; **(d)** C; **(e)** B

Listening Task 6

(a) The mother

(b) The father

(c) The father

(d) The mother

(e) The father

(f) The mother

(g) The father

(h) The father

(i) The mother

Listening Task 7

(a) Three hours

(b) 500 euros

(c) Hotel

(d) Overpricing

(e) Look at the price on the door.

(f) 10pm

(g) Seafood

(h) Credit card

Listening Task 8

(a) E; **(b)** D; **(c)** F; **(d)** A; **(e)** B

Reading Task 1

(a) réservé

(b) centre-ville

(c) garer

(d) peu

(e) l'escalier

(f) supplément

Reading Task 2

(a) (i) Paying

(ii) 8.00 to 18.00.

(iii) Every day except Sundays and holidays

(iv) Take a ticket

(b) It is the fire service exit

(c) In front of the town hall

Reading Task 3

(a) To invite Peter to France

(b) His uncle

(c) Two weeks

(d) (i)–(iii) In any order: empty bins; serve in the shop; clean the tents

(e) Translating for British campers.

(f) There are lots of students.

(g) (i) Spain

(ii) Hire car

(h) Send a text message

Reading Task 4

(a) D; **(b)** A; **(c)** C; **(d)** B; **(e)** D; **(f)** A

CHAPTER 5

Listening Task 1
(a) A; **(b)** B; **(c)** C; **(d)** A; **(e)** B; **(f)** B
Listening Task 2
Monique: F and H
Claude: C and I
Sylvie: D and G
Marc: D and E
Listening Task 3

Reading Task 1
(a) 4; **(b)** 6; **(c)** 1; **(d)** 3; **(e)** 5; **(f)** 2
Reading Task 2
(a) quartier; **(b)** sortes; **(c)** brique; **(d)** carton; **(e)** crimes;
(f) enfants; **(g)** plastique; **(h)** joue
Reading Task 3
(a) Burglaries
(b) The garage
(c) Leave on a light
(d) (i)–(ii) In any order: the phone number of your hotel; a key
(e) They can remove post from the letterbox.
(f) Car keys
(g) A burglar alarm
(h) Strangers
(i) Sums of money
(j) Jewellery
Reading Task 4
(a) Dordogne
(b) Gard
(c) Paris
(d) Champagne
Reading Task 5
(a) Protecting the environment
(b) Spread litter
(c) The number of drivers
(d) Take the train.
(e) Revive the flora and fauna.
(f) Written letters

CHAPTER 6
Listening Task 1
(a) She doesn't get on with him.
    (i)–(iv) Any four from: he criticised her; he scolded her; he
    punished her; his discipline is bad; the students chat;
    nobody listens; nobody learns anything
(b) He thinks he is the best teacher.
    (i)–(iv) In any order: there was total silence; his discipline
    is excellent; he is an expert; he knows everything
(c) The teacher arrived 10 minutes late.
(d) He was sad and did not smile.
(e) It is as if they are talking about two different teachers.
Listening Task 2
(a) It was too far to walk and his family could not afford the

bus fares.
(b) He makes toys.
(c) Send his brother to school
(d) It is too far or families prefer to see their children working
on the farm.
Listening Task 3
(a) Laudic; **(b)** 16; **(c)** Chemistry; **(d)** Nurse; **(e)** Leclerc;
(f) 17; **(g)** Geography; **(h)** Engineer
Listening Task 4
(a) Farm work
(b) A fear of animals
(c) French
(d) 5 June
(e) 28 August
(f) Five
(g) Free
(h) 220 euros
Listening Task 5
(a) A; **(b)** B; **(c)** C; **(d)** B; **(e)** A
Listening Task 6
(a) C
(b) She wanted to chat.
(c) He got a mechanic.
(d) A road accident
(e) C
Listening Task 7
(a) False; **(b)** True; **(c)** False; **(d)** True; **(e)** False;
(f) True; **(g)** False **(h)** False; **(i)** False; **(j)** False
Reading Task 1
(a) Thursday and Sunday
(b) August
(c) The town hall
(d) The fourth stop
(e) On the ground floor
(f) A tie
(g) Jewellery
Reading Task 2
(a) A bouncer
(b) A night club in a dangerous part of Marseille.
(c) About 50
(d) 2000
(e) (i)–(iii) In any order: she is the youngest; she is the
smallest; she is the bravest.
(f) Mobile phone
(g) Solidarity with male bouncers.
(h) A single mother
(i) Because of her job
(j) House husband
(k) Search a woman
(l) Unemployment
Reading Task 3
(a) (i)–(iv) In any order: make the beds; vacuum; cook; serve
in the bar
(b) Interesting but tiring
(c) An hour
(d) £6 an hour
(e) Tips
(f) The same job in the same hotel
(g) If she wants to go with her

Translated passages

CHAPTER 1

Speaking 1

Student: At last the great adventure was going to begin. All the team assembled very early in the morning and we left England by coach – from in front of the school – at six in the morning and after a long journey we arrived at 4pm, very tired, and my friend was waiting for us at the school. During the journey, I read and listened to music. Straight away, on our arrival, we went to his house by car. His father was driving. His house was small but comfortable. There was a small charming garden with flowers and a lawn. It was like a typical British garden, but not as pretty.

Teacher: Were you hungry?

Student: Yes, I ate a ham sandwich and I drank a glass of lemonade. After sleeping a little, we went out to train. We did exercises and practised with the ball. Then we went back and I spent the evening watching TV and chatting to my friend. Later, we went to a café to drink a glass of lemonade and to chat to our French friends. The atmosphere was marvellous. The next day, my French friend rejoined his friends. It was nice weather and the sun was shining. It was really too hot for a game of football. We went to the municipal stadium for the big match. At 3pm, the match began. At half-time, the British side was winning 2–0 and I had scored one of the goals from a free kick. But just after half-time, what a disaster! I got injured.

Teacher: What happened?

Student: One of the French players was angry because his team was losing and his tackle was very violent. I broke my leg. The pain was incredible. My team-mates were not happy either. My teacher called for an ambulance and it arrived ten minutes later. I stayed in hospital for three days and my friends came to see me every day. The hospital was very pleasant and the nurses looked after me very well.

Teacher: Did your team-mates bring you presents?

Student: Yes, they brought me fruit, chocolate and books. The whole French team came to see me. The violent player said sorry. He gave me a gold watch as a present. His parents wrote to my parents to say sorry. I think that my visit to France was a disaster and I will never go back there.

Writing 1

Interview with Isabelle Frétey – international star

Everybody has heard of Isabelle: the best female tennis player in France. By the age of 24 she had already won three competitions and this summer she is going to try to win Wimbledon. A pretty Parisian, she is a true star. But her life has not always been easy.

– Isabelle, tell us about your childhood.

– Life was hard. What a nightmare! My parents died when I was three and I went to live with my aunt in a rough suburb of Paris. There were no tennis courts. To play, I had to travel by tube for an hour. But at last I found a good club. I had been a member for a year when I met Marcel, who is now my trainer and my husband.

– And what do you do to stay fit?

– The important thing is to eat well. I never drink alcohol, I don't smoke and I exercise. And I play tennis with Marcel for four hours a day.

– And your first success?

– I won my first tournament in the USA. I was so happy. After winning, we celebrated our success with a meal in a five-star restaurant.

– Apart from tennis, what do you like to do?

– I love reading. When I get home, I like to settle in an armchair and read a novel.

– And your family?

– I am an only child and my aunt is dead. But I have Marcel, my husband, and one day we hope to have children. But before having children, I want to win more tournaments. I must go to Wimbledon and I must win.

– And the problems of the world?

– For me, the main problem is the environment. The world is not focussing on what is happening. We are in the process of destroying the planet.

– Isabelle, good luck at Wimbledon.

– Thank you.

Writing 2

Dear Madeleine,

I have been in hospital for two days. Three days ago, as it was nice, I decided to go for a long walk in the countryside near my house. My older brother accompanied me.

Suddenly, the weather changed. A storm! It started to rain. Soon, it was pouring and I was soaked to the skin. And I was cold too. What a disaster! While trying to get home as quickly as possible, unfortunately I slipped in the mud and I fell. How awful! I broke my leg and my arm. The pain was awful! Immediately, my brother phoned for an ambulance. After ringing, my brother gave me his coat and I felt less cold. Without him, I would be dead. The ambulance arrived five minutes later and I told the ambulance people what had happened. Ten minutes later, I had arrived at the hospital.

Here in hospital, I have already read two books and I listen to music. The nurses are nice and the food is good. They give me everything I ask for. I think that the hospitals in France are the best in the world because the food is so good and the doctors always have the time to do what they have to, whereas in England the doctors always seem so rushed. I can choose what I want. Yesterday, I ate steak and chips and even drank some wine! I am happy because I am going to leave hospital tomorrow. All's well that ends well. But I won't go for any more walks in the country. I will have to take my walks in the park.

See you soon, Paula

CHAPTER 2

Speaking 1

Teacher: Do you smoke?

Student: Absolutely not. It is so bad for your health. In the past, I smoked regularly. I was hooked on cigarettes but after seeing a film on the dangers of smoking, I stopped. I have completely given up cigarettes, and I don't smoke anymore. I haven't smoked for two years.

Teacher: Why?

Student: Tobacco contains substances that are dangerous for the heart, skin and especially the lungs, so I have no desire to start again. The latest figures are frightening. Now, there are more girls than boys who smoke. Three girls out of ten smoke. Despite the advice of my parents, my sister smokes and it stinks. Her clothes smell bad and her teeth and fingers are yellow. It is so disgusting. But she says she is about to stop.

Teacher: And the government?

Student: They have banned tobacco advertising. They have banned adverts for tobacco on TV. Cigarette manufacturers try to attract young people. The multinationals even encourage youngsters to smoke. In Africa, they give out free cigarettes. What a scandal! What a nightmare! Unfortunately, cigarette manufacturers finance Formula 1, and youngsters can see cigarette advertising on TV. The government must do more to help and protect young people. They should increase the price of cigarettes.

Teacher: Why do so many youngsters smoke?

Student: They smoke to look more grown up. There are people who smoke to be like their friends. They do it to look sophisticated. They like to smoke when they are with their friends. They say that cigarettes calm their nerves. They find it relaxing and that it combats stress. If there is a problem, without delay, they take out cigarettes.

Teacher: And passive smoking?

Student: When I see people smoking, I get angry. Passive smoking worries me. I am a victim of passive smoking, I have become asthmatic. Nobody has the right to make others suffer.

Teacher: Do you have any advice to give children?

Student: Yes. Before starting to smoke, think! It is the worst thing that you can do. If you smoke, you are going to regret it.

Writing 1

I am going to describe my future. I am going to be really happy! It will be in a year, in five years or perhaps when I am sixty, but it is happiness that I am looking for. I will be happy because I will lead my life the way that I have chosen. I would like to get married.

I will not get married before 30 and I will have at least three children. Being a parent is part of my plans although I am frightened of having children. I want babies, lots, lots, but before getting married I want to travel all over the world. After seeing the world, the important thing is love. I will live in a luxury house because when I leave school, I hope to find a good partner. When I meet him/her, I will know straight away if it is the person for me. When I finish my studies, perhaps I will marry a celebrity. I will be a house husband/wife. My partner will continue working while I will stay at home. I am the one who will look after the children at home.

For me, marriage is important to the couple's relationship. It is the bond that unites the couple. I am going to get married because it is important for children to have stability. For a child, stability is the most important thing. I have just discussed this subject with my sister. My sister says that she does not understand why people get married. How awful! She says that it is simpler to co-habit without getting married. She is about to go and live with her boyfriend. I will never co-habit despite the fact that my parents had co-habited before they got married. They had been co-habiting for five years. My brother is neither for nor against marriage and he does not want children unfortunately.

CHAPTER 3

Speaking 1

Teacher: What do you like doing?

Student: What I like most is sport. I like all sports, but my favourite sport is tennis. I have been playing tennis for ten years, that is to say nearly all my life. My parents encouraged me because they also play. I decided to become a member of a club when I was eight and I have just won my first competition.

Teacher: Do you do another sport?

Student: I am about to join a horse-riding club. I was given a horse last year. How marvellous! It is the most beautiful horse in the world. It is so intelligent. I began to ride when I was ten, but I had stopped because I had neither a horse nor money.

Teacher: What other activity do you like?

Student: I love the cinema and films. On Saturday evenings, I absolutely must go to the cinema. My younger brother comes with me. Before going, we look for the best films on the Internet. After finding a good film, we go and see it in town. My brother likes horror films, whereas I like drama films.

Teacher: Do you like reading?

Student: When I have finished my homework in the evening, I always want to read. Without delay, I get my novel and I read. I never switch on the TV. So many programmes are so stupid! What a waste of time! My brother watches just anything on TV despite the fact that most programmes are stupid…

Writing 1

What I like most is the security that the mobile offers. You are never alone with a mobile and you can really easily call the police if you need to. Before going out, I always tell my parents that they can call me anytime. That reassures them. With my new mobile, I can now do research for my homework because I can surf the Internet. To amuse myself, I send e-mails, I download video clips and I play games. It is useful, it doesn't make any noise and my mobile has a five-megapixel camera that I can use at the scene of an accident or a crime.

We have the Internet at school – it is marvellous. It is an excellent way of communicating with everyone. It is useful for contacting young people throughout the world. It helps us to find contacts and allows us to practise another language. For me, the social element is important. I love music and I have an MP3 player which is so light, with a touch screen.

But I have decided there are disadvantages. Too many people spend too much time on their computers. They do less sport and after spending so much time in front of the screen they have eyesight problems. They are no longer interested in anything, except computers. They want to eat fast-food in front of the screen. They begin to get more lonely, even morose. Friends are no longer important to them. What a disaster! To save these people, you have to limit access to the computer.

Mobiles are dangerous for your health. Scientists cannot agree amongst themselves. Be careful! Young people, ignoring the teacher, write texts during lessons. I have a girl friend who has been in contact with a stranger for a long time. What a bad idea! I need my mobile, I would be lost without it, but at the end of the month the bill is so dear.

CHAPTER 4

Speaking 1

Student: Last year, I decided to go on holiday in June with my older brother. I wanted to visit my friends in Switzerland. They have been living there for two years. What a good idea! I think that Switzerland is the most beautiful country in the world because the countryside and the mountains are superb!

Teacher: What was the weather like?

Student: It was nice weather and we went to the airport by taxi. We got on the plane, I put on my safety belt and the plane took off. I wasn't afraid.

Teacher: What did you do during the flight?

Student: Before leaving, I had bought a novel. I played cards and I read. We had lunch, but the meal was not very good. It was chicken, and I didn't like it. After eating, I didn't feel well. I arrived in Switzerland at six in the evening and my friends were waiting for me at the airport. They were very kind. On the way to the house, we crossed the city of Geneva, we admired the lake and then reached the house. On arriving, we ate. The meal was delicious. Then we went to bed.

Teacher: And your impressions?

Student: I think that the journey went well and that my friends were very nice.

Teacher: What will you do next year?

Student: I must return to Switzerland to ski. I would like to ski because I love skiing and the snow is so good in Verbier. I would also like to go horse-riding because I have a horse here in England and I like horse-riding in spite of the snow. Last year in Verbier, I went on rides in the mountains and I would like to do the same thing this year because I really liked it. There is a skating rink and a swimming pool in Verbier.

Writing 1

I am going to describe my stay in Blackpool. I have just spent two unforgettable weeks there. For me, Blackpool is the best city in England for holidays because there is always something to do. I was staying in a five-star hotel because my parents had won the lottery. It was superb because the swimming pool was always really empty! What luxury! They won a fortune so now we have bought a superb car and we stay in the best hotels. Fortunately, my younger sister refused to come with us because she doesn't like Blackpool. She went to visit my grandmother. In the mornings, I walked on the beach. In the afternoons, I played football in the park and in the evenings I went out with my parents. I have to do a lot of exercise to keep fit.

One day, I decided to go to a theme park. On arriving, I saw the queues. It was terrible because the queues were so long. After waiting two hours, I was not happy. I was about to ask for my money back. I won't go to theme parks anymore.

In my opinion, the stay was excellent because we had a very good time all the time and I was lucky enough to meet a handsome boy/a pretty girl. I went out with him/her and we got on so well. It was fine weather every day. I would go back there without hesitating despite the long queues.

In summer, I will go to the USA and I will see my older brother. He has been living there for two years. I would like to see New York and he will come with me. I want to travel across the country to get to know it better. My brother will hire a car and off we go!

CHAPTER 5

Speaking 1

Teacher: What problems are there environmentally?

Student: We mistreat the Earth. What a disaster! Every year the situation gets worse. The people living in the northern countries use enormous amounts of energy. Each of us consumes the equivalent of ten tonnes of coal a year. Man is an endangered species. We burn the forests that consume CO_2. In Brazil, they have burned thousands of square kilometres in a year. We pollute the air, we poison our rivers and our seas, we treat the planet like a dustbin, we modify plants and animals, we bury nuclear waste and we destroy natural resources. The ozone layer is disappearing because of exhaust fumes. That causes the greenhouse effect and global warming. The greenhouse effect is a vicious circle. We produce toxic gases that rise in the atmosphere. The heat of the Sun rises, but is blocked by the gases. The Earth becomes hotter and hotter. The seas rise and lots of species are endangered. Our energy consumption is too high and the planet suffers.

Teacher: And what about flooding?

Student: The snow melts, the rain falls, the rivers overflow, the fields are flooded, and the streets are under water. People are forced to leave their homes, the houses are ruined, the countryside is devastated and thousands of people are dead. Soon we will no longer have any fossil fuels.

Teacher: And the answer?

Student: Governments close their eyes to the problem. We have to change our habits, and we have to have an action plan. We don't have much time left. We need to plant trees to replace the burnt forests. We must use public transport to reduce pollution. We should take showers, not baths, to safeguard the Earth's resources and to reduce water consumption. We must recycle everything. We must use solar panels, install double glazing and insulate our homes. We should use bicycles to reduce CO_2 emissions and to reduce petrol consumption. The car represents liberty but also pollution. If we didn't use the car, we would use less petrol. If we used the bus and the train, we would no longer pollute the atmosphere, we would breathe clean air, we would do more exercise, we would be less stressed and we would feel better.

Writing 1

I do what I can to protect the environment. Despite our efforts, our planet is on the point of dying. What a disaster!

I walk or I cycle. I never get into a car. I have decided to use public transport. I never throw litter. I even pick up litter in the park.

I never waste energy. Before going out, I switch off lights and turn off taps. My parents have installed solar panels and double-glazing, and our house is really well insulated. After bathing or showering, I water the garden with the water I used.

When speaking to people, I encourage them to not use their car. The car represents liberty but also pollution. If we didn't use the car, we would use less petrol. If we took the bus and the train, we would no longer pollute the atmosphere, we would breathe clean air, we would do more exercise, we would be less stressed and we would feel better.

In my house we really do have to recycle. I recycle cardboard, paper, bottles, plastic and packaging. I re-use plastic bags. We make compost with organic waste. I use rechargable batteries to protect the environment. When I buy paper for example, I try to buy paper made from recycled materials. I give the clothes that I no longer wear to charity. Before buying something, I ask myself if I really need it.

I have written a letter to the Prime Minister. I told him that we should reduce the amount of packaging per product, create more recycling centres, create cycle paths everywhere in our cities, plant trees in the streets and improve public transport. On top of that, I told him to ban cars from town centres and to ban free plastic bags. We should build fewer new roads and airports as well.

CHAPTER 6

Speaking 1

Teacher: And what about your future plans?

Student: I have just done work experience and the experience has given me ideas for the future. I had to get up terribly early and I was working in an office. I had to photocopy documents, answer the phone, call customers and make the tea. As a result of this unfortunate experience, I have decided that I never want to work in an office.

Teacher: Why?

Student: Because the work was boring. Several times, I was on the point of leaving; the work was so boring. Despite the fact that my colleagues were nice, I was fed up with it. It wasn't the sort of work that I had been promised. The boss told me that I had to make the tea for the others. What a waste of time! It was an unforgettable experience. Fortunately, I have learned what I want to do and what I don't want to do.

Teacher: And that is?

Student: To start with, I am going to continue with my studies because I have seen that unqualified people have the worst things to do. Then I will go to university to get the necessary qualifications to work in a profession. I have decided I don't want to work in the open air all the time and that I don't want to work in an office either. I am certain that I don't want to become a teacher. It is true that I dreamt of becoming a celebrity, but I think I want to become a journalist because the work is interesting, it is well paid and I would work outside and inside.

Teacher: And what about marriage?

Student: I will not get married before the age of 30 and I will have three children. When I finish my studies, I hope to find a good partner. I will be happy because I will lead my life in the way that I have chosen. I will live in a luxurious house and I will continue to work whilst my partner stays at home.

Teacher: Marriage is important to you?

Student: Marriage is important to the couple's relationship. It is the bond that unites the couple. I am going to get married because it is important for children to have stability.

Writing 1

I am fed up with school. I am not receiving the education that had been promised to me. I have been a student here for four years. I find the school day very stressful and I am on the point of getting ill from it. I am just a name on a list and the rules are unreasonable. It is forbidden to wear make-up or jewellery, give our opinion, smoke, eat and drink in class etc, etc. When you get up, you have to put on an ugly, frightful uniform. Although it is good for discipline, it is ugly and not very elegant. Everybody looks the same. It is the worst school in the area. The atmosphere in my school is terrible. There is violence and graffiti. Extra-curricular activities do not exist. Some students make too much noise and I cannot hear the teacher. The football pitches are too small and there isn't enough equipment. What a disaster!

I do not get on very well with my teachers because they are not interested in me. They explain nothing, they do not listen to us and do not understand us. They give us too much homework. I have a language teacher who has no authority and who cannot prepare his lessons. I do not understand anything that is going on. Despite the fact that I haven't the time to do everything asked of me, my parents put me under pressure without thinking. We work all the time and do not have time for leisure. I must get good marks all the time. I fail everything, I do not make progress anymore and all my results are disastrous. I have decided to do A-levels but unfortunately to do them I need good marks. I would like to study in another school and I have just asked my parents if I can change schools.

Listening transcripts

CHAPTER 1

Speaking 1 (track 2)
Listening 1 (track 3)

Edgar: Jean, tu vas en Grèce?

Jean: Je voudrais passer les vacances en Grèce, tu sais, mais malheureusement je n'ai pas un sou et il faut qu'on reste ici à Lyon.

Edgar: Tu seras avec qui?

Jean: J'ai une copine qui habite ici. Elle ne part pas non plus.

Edgar: Tu aimes Lyon?

Jean: Lyon est une ville un peu trop tranquille...il n'y a pas grand-chose à faire ici.

Edgar: Qu'est-ce que tu vas faire ici?

Jean: Pour gagner de l'argent, pendant la journée, je vais aider un voisin à nettoyer son jardin. Le travail m'aidera à rester en bonne condition physique. Et le soir, je jouerai aux cartes avec ma copine.

Edgar: Moi, je vais en Espagne.

Jean: Si les vacances étaient plus longues, j'irais en Espagne. L'Espagne est un pays qui me plaît. L'année dernière, j'y ai passé mes vacances. J'y suis allé en auto-stop.

Edgar: Quel aspect de l'Espagne t'a plu?

Jean: Les saucisses et la bière étaient formidables!

Listening 2 (track 4)

1: Bonsoir. Donnez-moi une bière, s'il vous plaît, et un sandwich au fromage.

2: Je voudrais un café et une glace, s'il vous plaît.

3: Un jus d'orange, s'il vous plaît, et un hot-dog.

Listening 3 (track 5)

– Tu sais, il y a un an je pesais 90 kilos. Maintenant, je pèse 70 kilos. Et tu sais comment j'ai perdu tant de kilos? Alors c'est simple. J'ai cessé de fumer. Avant, je ne pouvais pas marcher 100 mètres sans me sentir fatigué. Maintenant je joue au badminton sans problème.

– Quand as-tu commencé à fumer?

– Il y a trois ans. J'étais dans un café et un client a laissé un paquet de cigarettes sur la table. Sans réfléchir, j'ai fumé une cigarette. Un mois plus tard, j'en fumais une quarantaine par jour. Mais un jour j'ai vu une émission sur les maladies provoquées par le tabac. J'ai vu les victimes à l'hôpital. Je ne veux pas de ça. Le lendemain j'ai fumé vingt cigarettes, le lendemain dix cigarettes, le lendemain cinq cigarettes, puis j'y ai renoncé complètement.

– Alors ta vie a changé?

– Oui, et les choses vont beaucoup mieux avec mon amie Anne. Elle ne supportait pas l'odeur du tabac. Lorsqu'on parlait dans un café, elle restait toujours à deux mètres de moi. Maintenant, elle s'asseoit à côté de moi.

Listening 4 (track 6)

Elise: Ecoute Pierre, je ne peux pas sortir avec toi ce soir. J'ai mal là...là...entre les yeux.

Pierre: Mais, qu'est-ce qui a causé ça?

Elise: Alors, hier soir j'ai dîné au restaurant. Normalement, je ne supporte pas le poisson mais j'en ai mangé quand même. Que je suis bête!

Pierre: Mais ça fait deux fois cette semaine que tu me dis que tu es malade. Ce mal est encore un prétexte?

Elise: Pierre, je vais me coucher tout de suite et on sortira demain. Je te le promets.

Pierre: Eh, j'ai déjà entendu ce genre de promesses. On verra.

Elise: Fais-moi une bise, Pierre.

CHAPTER 2

Speaking 1 (track 7)
Listening 1 (track 8)

1: – Elle est comment, ta famille?

– C'est un peu comme tout le monde, je crois. J'ai un petit frère de dix ans. Il est assez sympa mais il m'énerve, des fois. Il fait beaucoup de bruit et il est toujours dans ma chambre. Il adore le cyclisme et pour son anniversaire il a reçu un vélo.

2: – Et tes parents?

– Ils sont vraiment sympa. Je suis presque adulte et ils l'acceptent. J'ai le droit de sortir en ville et d'acheter mes propres vêtements. L'année prochaine, j'irai en vacances avec mes copines. Ce sera chouette.

Listening 2 (track 9)

1: – Audrey Tautou, comment était votre enfance?

– Mon enfance a été très heureuse. Je faisais beaucoup d'activités: piano, chant, dessin et sport. J'ai un frère et deux sœurs, et je les adore. On ne se voit pas très souvent, mais les liens sont très forts.

2: – Comment avez-vous décidé de devenir actrice?

– Après mes examens, mes parents m'ont offert comme cadeau un stage d'été, des cours de théâtre pour apprendre un peu le métier d'actrice. Cela m'a beaucoup plu, et j'ai continué dans ce métier. Le jour du casting de mon premier film, *Vénus Beauté*, je suis arrivée une heure en retard – je me suis perdue dans Paris. Heureusement, ils m'ont invitée à revenir le lendemain, et ils m'ont offert le rôle. Le film a eu un grand succès.

3: – Et le film *Amélie Poulain*?

– J'ai eu beaucoup de chance qu'on me propose le rôle d'Amélie. Je pense que je ressemble à Amélie dans la mesure où j'étais une enfant qui aimait beaucoup la fantaisie. C'est ce film qui m'a rendue célèbre. L'idée d'être si bien connue est difficile pour moi. Je n'aime pas me voir dans un magazine. Je veux que ma vie reste privée.

Listening 3 (track 10)

– Qu'en pensez-vous, Monsieur Laudic?

– Je n'accepte pas ce que vous dites. En fait, je pense que vous dites des bêtises. L'idée de donner de l'argent aux chômeurs est ridicule. Les chômeurs...ce sont des paresseux et ils ne méritent rien.

– Qu'en pensez-vous, Madame Bernard?

– Je crois qu'on fait des progrès. Il y a moins de pauvreté dans notre ville, les gens semblent plus contents, et à mon avis l'avenir est plein d'espoir. Oui, les choses vont beaucoup mieux.

– Votre opinion, Monsieur Renault?

– Alors, quand je vois le monde tel qu'il est, j'ai envie de pleurer. Il y a tant de gens tristes, tant de chômeurs, tant de tragédies tous les jours dans les journaux. Les choses deviennent de pire en pire. Qu'est-ce qu'on peut faire?

CHAPTER 3

Speaking 1 (track 11)
Listening 1 (track 12)

Bonsoir, c'est Marie. Je veux laisser un message pour Angélique. Le film commence à vingt heures trente, alors on se retrouve chez Michelle à dix-neuf heures trente. On va au cinéma dans la voiture de Michelle. Paul n'a pas d'argent et ne vient pas. Alain travaille ce soir, mais il nous retrouvera au café après le film.

Listening 2 (track 13)

Allô, Luc? Ici Jean-Paul. Mon numéro de téléphone est le zéro-trois, vingt-deux, trente-huit, cinquante-six, vingt-quatre. J'ai la grippe et je ne peux pas venir à vingt heures comme prévu. Demain jeudi non plus, mais vendredi c'est bon. J'ai acheté du parfum pour ta sœur pour la remercier. Si on sortait? Je vous invite à manger de la cuisine italienne avec moi. À bientôt.

Listening 3 (track 14)

(a) Hier soir il y a eu un drame à la Banque Nationale de Paris à Tours. Deux hommes masqués se sont échappés avec un million d'euros. La gendarmerie cherche toujours les malfaiteurs.

(b) Il y aura beaucoup d'ambiance ce soir au stade national pour la rencontre de l'équipe espagnole et de l'équipe allemande dans la finale de la coupe.

(c) Il pleut toujours dans le Midi, et les inondations ont provoqué des dizaines de morts et des dégâts importants. Dans quelques endroits l'eau est d'une profondeur de dix mètres.

(d) Le premier ministre britannique est arrivé à Paris ce matin pour des entretiens avec le premier ministre français sur la crise en Afrique.

(e) Gros embouteillage sur la N10 entre Tours et Angers à la suite d'une collision entre un camion et une voiture.

Listening 4 (track 15)

Juliette: Alors Marc, quelle sorte de personne cherches-tu comme correspondant?

Marc: Je veux qu'il soit comme moi, c'est-à-dire qu'il aime voyager, qu'il aime parler des langues étrangères.

Juliette: Tu veux une personne sportive?

Marc: Moi, j'aime bien le sport, mais je préfère les passe-temps plus calmes, la lecture, la musique classique.

Juliette: Tu as d'autres passe-temps?

Marc: Chez moi j'ai environ deux mille timbres, une centaine de papillons et des tiroirs pleins de cartes postales. Alors Juliette, quelle sorte de personne cherches-tu?

Juliette: Je veux qu'elle soit comme moi. Je veux une personne enthousiaste qui aime bouger, sortir, faire des choses.

Marc: Tu veux une personne sportive?

Juliette: Pour moi, le sport est la chose la plus importante de ma vie. Sans le sport, je serais perdue.

Marc: Tu as d'autres occupations?

Juliette: Je vais souvent à la messe et j'aide le prêtre à faire son travail quand je peux.

Listening 5 (track 16)

Le cinéma Rex annonce une séance spéciale. La première du film américain en version originale aura lieu mardi à vingt heures. Ouvert à tout le monde. Entrée sept euros. Il n'est pas nécessaire de réserver. Téléphonez au 03 23 95 67 44.

Listening 6 (track 17)

(a) Aujourd'hui. Promotion spéciale. Jambon, saucisson, pâté. Réductions jusqu'à vingt pour cent.

(b) Cette semaine. Promotion spéciale. Jupes, chemisiers, robes. Réductions de dix pour cent.

(c) Pendant deux semaines. Offre spéciale. Réductions de dix pour cent sur les pommes, les haricots, les bananes et les choux.

Listening 7 (track 18)

Venez au Restaurant Gilbert situé en face de la mairie. C'est le seul restaurant belge de la ville. Notre menu du jour est à quinze euros, boisson comprise. Le service est aussi compris. Aujourd'hui, le plat du jour est le steak frites. Nous sommes ouverts tous les jours sauf le mardi.

Listening 8 (track 19)

– Qu'est-ce que tu fais le dimanche matin?

– Comme tous les jours je prends ma douche à sept heures et demie, puis à huit heures je mange un peu de pain et je bois un café.

– Et après?

– À huit heures et demie je fais du jogging, et à neuf heures j'ouvre mes livres et je travaille pendant une heure. À dix heures je vais à la messe, à onze heures je vais voir un copain, et à onze heures et demie on sort. On aime bien faire un tour le long de la rivière. À midi on va manger chez moi.

CHAPTER 4

Speaking 1 (track 20)

Listening 1 (track 21)

Le train en provenance de Bourges arrivera au quai numéro trois à dix-neuf heures. Dans le train, il y a un wagon-restaurant et pour les passagers qui ont des vélos, veuillez vous présenter au contrôleur.

Listening 2 (track 22)

Visite guidée du musée, tous les mercredis à quatorze heures. Vous pouvez acheter votre ticket à l'entrée du musée. Durée de la visite: une heure et demie.

Listening 3 (track 23)

– Alors, tu as passé de bonnes vacances en Espagne?

– Mon mari n'était pas content. La cuisine, les gens, le cinéma, les maisons, le climat, le transport. Tout était affreux pour lui.

– Et qu'est-ce que tu penses de ces choses-là?

– Je suis d'accord avec lui. La cuisine était trop grasse et la plupart des plats manquaient de finesse. Ils mangent trop d'ail, les Espagnols.

– Et les gens?

– On a connu tant de gens sympa qu'il est difficile de comprendre l'opinion de mon mari. Je ne suis pas de son avis. Les Espagnols sont des gens gais et généreux.

– Et le cinéma?

– J'ai été ravie des films espagnols. Nous sommes allés au cinéma tous les jours. Il y avait tant de choix et les films étaient meilleurs que les nôtres.

– Et les maisons?

– Alors là, j'ai été franchement déçue. La plupart des gens habitent des appartements au centre-ville. Ils n'ont pas de jardin, ils n'ont pas de garage. J'ai trouvé ça triste.

– Et le climat?

– La plupart du temps il a fait beaucoup trop chaud. J'ai dû rester à l'ombre. Non, je préfère le climat français.

– Et le transport?

– J'avais entendu dire beaucoup de mal des transports espagnols, mais franchement les trains étaient propres et à l'heure – pas comme en France – les autobus étaient bien organisés, et il y avait des taxis partout.

Listening 4 (track 24)

(a) Votre train arrivera à Paris à quinze heures vingt.

(b) Vous voulez une chambre? Je vous propose une chambre à 50 euros.

(c) La chambre est pour une personne. Elle a un lit et une baignoire.

(d) Vous voulez aller au centre-ville? Vous pouvez y aller à pied.

(e) Au centre-ville, il y a un très joli monument. C'est la cathédrale. Son architecture est très intéressante.

Listening 5 (track 25)

– Sandra, où es-tu allée en vacances?

– On a fait du camping. On est allé au camping de la forêt.

– Pourquoi ce camping-là?

– Parce que dans la forêt il faisait frais.

– Qu'est-ce que tu as fait de bien?

– Tout était très bien: la piscine, les restaurants, la plage, mais ce que j'ai préféré, c'était le bal chaque soir.

– Vous avez loué une voiture?

– Non, parce que nous avions des vélos. Nous sommes allés partout à vélo.

– Et le temps?

– Il a fait une chaleur étouffante.

Listening 6 (track 26)

La mère: Moi, je veux aller à Londres en voiture et prendre le ferry. Quelquefois, j'ai le mal de mer, mais normalement tout va bien, et j'aime manger dans le restaurant à bord du bateau.

Le père: Mais non. Le voyage est beaucoup plus rapide si on prend l'avion. On sera à Londres en deux heures. Et tu sais que tu as presque toujours le mal de mer. C'est moi qui n'ai jamais eu le mal de mer. Et la cuisine à bord du bateau est affreuse.

La mère: Mais si on prend l'avion, on ne voit rien. Si on prend la voiture, on voit le nord de la France, et on voit le sud de l'Angleterre. Et la traversée est si jolie. De l'avion on ne voit que des nuages.

Le père: Ma chérie, l'avion est plus rapide!

La mère: L'aéroport est si loin du centre-ville. Oui, on arrive à Londres en deux heures, mais il faut encore deux heures pour arriver à notre hôtel.

Le père: Bon. Je crois que j'ai trouvé la solution. On va prendre le train par le tunnel. Il y a des pannes de temps en temps, mais tu ne vas pas avoir le mal de mer.

La mère: C'est vrai, et le train par le tunnel sous la Manche arrivera directement à Londres. Oui, on fait comme ça.

Listening 7 (track 27)

Offre spéciale. On vous propose un week-end en Espagne. Visitez Madrid, capitale pittoresque, historique et inoubliable. Le vol charter part de Paris à dix-huit heures et arrive à Madrid à vingt et une heures. Le prix? 500 euros. Mais attention, parce que le prix de l'hôtel n'est pas compris. Il est facile de trouver un bon hôtel au centre-ville, mais on vous demandera le double du vrai prix de la chambre. La solution est de regarder sur la porte même de votre chambre. Il y aura un avis qui donne le vrai prix. En ce qui concerne les restaurants en Espagne, il faut savoir que le soir les repas ne commencent pas avant vingt-deux heures. Vous allez manger des omelettes, de la paella, mais aussi sans doute le plat inoubliable de Madrid: les fruits de mer. Téléphonez tout de suite et ayez à votre disposition votre carte de crédit.

Listening 8 (track 28)

Professeur: Alors, nous sommes à Londres depuis une semaine maintenant, n'est-ce pas? Que pensez-vous de la capitale britannique? Toi, Carine, tu veux commencer? Que penses-tu de Londres?

Carine: Eh ben, Londres, c'est assez bien je trouve. Enfin, c'est pas mal. Je dois dire qu'il y a beaucoup à voir, les musées, les théâtres, les cinémas, les magasins, les parcs et tout ça. Eh oui, il y a une énorme variété d'endroits à visiter.

Professeur: Et toi, François?

François: Pour moi, vous voyez, qui viens de la campagne, je trouve que Londres est très bruyant. J'aime la ville, mais toutes ces voitures, ces taxis, tout ce monde, ce n'est que du bruit et de la fumée. L'air est sale!

Professeur: Stéphanie, qu'est-ce que tu penses de Londres?

Stéphanie: Ah, c'est sympa. On peut parler avec les gens et ils répondent. Ils sont accueillants, chaleureux, pas comme à Paris où je trouve que les gens sont assez froids en général.

Professeur: Et toi, Caroline? Qu'est-ce que tu penses de Londres?

Caroline: Bof! Il y a des choses assez bien comme les parcs, mais il y a d'autres choses que je n'aime pas du tout. Le métro par exemple. Ah, ce n'est pas comme à Paris. C'est difficile à dire. Je ne sais pas, moi. C'est pas mal, je suppose.

Professeur: Merci, Caroline. Et toi, finalement, Christophe. Tu aimes Londres?

Christophe: Ah, c'est passionnant, Londres. C'est une ville que j'aimerais visiter très, très souvent. C'est chouette, hein? J'ai passé une semaine formidable ici.

CHAPTER 5

Speaking 1 (track 29)

Listening 1 (track 30)

1: – Pardon, monsieur, pour aller à la piscine?
– Ce n'est pas loin. Allez tout droit.
2: – Madame, pouvez-vous m'aider? Je cherche l'église Saint Jean.
– Oui, monsieur, il faut prendre la première rue à gauche.
3: – Pardon, monsieur, la plage, c'est dans quelle direction?
– Eh bien, madame, vous devez traverser la place puis continuer tout droit.

Listening 2 (track 31)

Anne: Monique, qu'est-ce que tu fais à la maison?

Monique: Une chose que je ne fais pas, c'est laver la voiture. Cela m'ennuie. Mais tous les jours, je prépare le repas du soir et je fais les lits. Claude, qu'est-ce que tu fais à la maison?

Claude: Je passe l'aspirateur de temps en temps. J'aime bien faire ça. Je nettoie un peu aussi. Mais, une chose que je ne fais jamais, c'est le repassage. Et toi, Sylvie, qu'est-ce que tu fais à la maison?

Sylvie: J'adore faire le jardinage. Ça détend. Et je fais la vaisselle. Mais par contre je ne supporte pas les grandes surfaces. Je refuse de faire les courses. Et toi, Marc, qu'est-ce que tu fais à la maison?

Marc: Ma mère me demande de faire les lits et de nettoyer ma chambre, mais je ne le fais pas. En revanche, une chose que je fais, c'est la vaisselle. Et j'aime bien aussi laver la voiture.

Listening 3 (track 32)

Voici la météo pour aujourd'hui. Dans le Nord, un vent va souffler très fort toute la journée. Dans le Sud, il fera très chaud, beaucoup plus chaud qu'hier. Dans l'Est, il fera du brouillard et ce sera très dangereux sur les routes. Dans l'Ouest, il fera très froid, les températures vont baisser rapidement. Dans le centre du pays, on attend un jour de pluie. Il va pleuvoir toute la journée.

CHAPTER 6

Speaking 1 (track 33)

Listening 1 (track 34)

Marc: Ecoute, Monique, que penses-tu du nouveau professeur?

Monique: Alors, Marc. Ça, c'est facile. Ça ne va pas du tout entre lui et moi. J'ai eu deux cours avec lui et il m'a grondée, il m'a critiquée et il m'a punie.

Marc: Mais moi aussi j'ai eu deux cours avec lui et je trouve qu'il est le meilleur professeur du collège. Et il m'a dit que je suis très fort en géographie.

Monique: Mais Marc, sa discipline est nulle. Les élèves bavardent pendant le cours, personne ne l'écoute, on n'apprend rien.

Marc: Monique, ce n'est pas vrai. Pendant mes cours avec lui, il y a un silence absolu. Sa discipline est excellente et aussi il est vraiment expert en sa matière. Il sait tout.

Monique: Marc, il ne sait rien. En plus, il n'arrive pas à répondre aux questions les plus simples.

Marc: Monique, il arrive toujours à l'heure tandis que les autres profs arrivent cinq, dix minutes en retard.

Monique: Mais mon ami, ce matin, il est arrivé dix minutes en retard. Il avait l'air triste pendant tout le cours et il n'a pas souri...même pas une fois.

Marc: J'ai l'impression qu'on parle de deux professeurs différents.

Listening 2 (track 35)

J'ai fait la connaissance d'un petit garçon, Alexandre, âgé de 12 ans. Sa famille ne pouvait pas lui payer le bus, et pendant quelque temps, il est allé à l'école à pied. Mais, dix kilomètres à pied, trois heures de marche tous les matins, c'était trop. Donc il ne va plus à l'école. Alexandre est surnommé 'Monsieur l'ingénieur', car il fabrique des jouets, par exemple, un petit vélo, une petite moto ou alors une voiture miniature, qu'il vend à des touristes. Avec l'argent qu'il gagne, il espère payer l'école à son petit frère. Les enfants qui vont à l'école sont des privilégiés: seulement 30% à peu près des enfants sont scolarisés. Beaucoup habitent trop loin et, pour d'autres, les familles préfèrent les voir travailler à la ferme.

Listening 3 (track 36)

1: – Bonjour, mademoiselle. Votre nom, s'il vous plaît.
– Bonjour, monsieur. Je m'appelle Sophie Laudic, L-A-U-D-I-C.
– Et vous avez quinze ans?
– Non, j'ai seize ans.
– Quelle est votre matière préférée au collège?
– Je préfère la chimie.
– Et qu'est-ce que vous voulez faire dans la vie?
– Je veux être infirmière.
2: – Bonjour, monsieur. Votre nom, s'il vous plaît.
– Bonjour, monsieur. Je m'appelle Paul Leclerc, L-E-C-L-E-R-C.
– Et vous avez quinze ans?
– Non, j'ai dix-sept ans.
– Quelle est votre matière préférée au collège?
– Je préfère la géographie.
– Et qu'est-ce que vous voulez faire dans la vie?
– Je veux devenir ingénieur.

Listening 4 (track 37)

Voulez-vous travailler dans une ferme cet été? Je cherche des jeunes gens qui n'ont pas peur des animaux, et qui parlent français. Vous travaillerez du 5 juin au 28 août, et vous ferez cinq heures par jour. Vous serez logé gratuitement à la ferme, et vous gagnerez 220 euros par semaine. Téléphonez maintenant.

Listening 5 (track 38)

Bonjour. Je suis le mari de Madame Ferrier qui travaille chez vous dans la section étrangère. Je suis désolé mais ma femme ne peut pas travailler aujourd'hui parce qu'elle a la grippe. Le médecin est avec elle maintenant. Mais elle dit qu'elle sera là demain sans faute.

Listening 6 (track 39)

Patron: En retard encore une fois?

Luc: Mais monsieur, ce n'est pas de ma faute.

Patron: Vous êtes arrivé en retard hier et avant-hier. Alors qu'est-ce qui vous est arrivé ce matin?

Luc: Ma mère m'a demandé de laisser des choses chez ma grand-mère. Comme ma grand-mère avait envie de bavarder, j'ai perdu vingt minutes.

Patron: Et après?

Luc: Je suis tombé en panne. J'ai fini par trouver un mécanicien, mais j'ai perdu encore une heure.

Patron: Et après?

Luc: Je me suis rendu compte que j'avais oublié tous mes papiers et j'ai dû repasser les prendre à la maison. J'ai encore perdu une demi-heure.

Patron: C'est tout?

Luc: Non. À dix minutes d'ici, il y a eu un accident de la route et j'ai dû attendre vingt minutes dans l'embouteillage.

Patron: Luc, la prochaine fois que vous arriverez en retard, je vais vous renvoyer.

Listening 7 (track 40)

– Jean-Pierre, il est facile de trouver du travail ici?
– Facile de trouver du travail ici? Je ne dis pas difficile de trouver du travail. Je dis impossible. Ça fait un an que je cherche du travail, mais je n'en ai pas trouvé. Je cherche du travail dans les fermes, tu sais, mais de nos jours tout se fait avec des machines. Cependant en automne j'arrive à trouver du travail. Dans les vergers. J'aide les agriculteurs à cueillir les pommes. À Paris, il serait plus facile de trouver du travail, mais ici je me plaît et j'ai plein d'amis. À Paris je ne connais personne. Et là-bas, la circulation est affreuse. Ici, dans ce village, il n'y a que quatre voitures. Nous avons deux magasins qui vendent les choses essentielles, mais pour s'acheter des vêtements par exemple, il faut aller à Paris.

Index

ACKNOWLEDGEMENTS

The author and publisher are grateful to the copyright holders for permission to use quoted materials and images.

©2009 Jupiterimages Corporation

Every effort has been made to trace copyright holders and obtain their permission for the use of copyright material. The author and publisher will gladly receive information enabling them to rectify any error or omission in subsequent editions. All facts are correct at time of going to press.

Letts Educational
4 Grosvenor Place
London SW1X 7DL

Orders: 015395 64910
Enquiries: 015395 65921
Email: enquiries@lettsandlonsdale.co.uk
Website: www.lettsandlonsdale.com

ISBN 9781906415792

01/100709

Published by Letts Educational Ltd

British Library Cataloguing in Publication Data.

A CIP record of this book is available from the British Library.

For Katie and Sam

Book Concept and Development: Helen Jacobs
Commissioning Editor: Rebecca Skinner
Author: Terry Murray
Project Editor: Richard Toms
Cover Design: Angela English
Text Design and Layout: Richard Arundale
Audio CD: Recorded and produced by Actors World Production Limited
Printed and bound in Italy

Letts Educational make every effort to ensure that all paper used in our books is made from wood pulp obtained from well-managed forests, controlled sources and recycled wood or fibre.

5 EASY WAYS TO ORDER

1. Visit our website:
   www.lettsandlonsdale.com
2. Fax your order to 015395 64167
3. Phone us on 015395 64910
4. Email us at orders@lettsandlonsdale.co.uk
5. Post your order to: Letts Educational,
   PO BOX 113, Holme, Carnforth, LA6 1WL

ESSENTIALS

The student-friendly approach to GCSE revision

REVISION GUIDES

WORKBOOKS

Get Essentials for your other subjects

DESIGN & TECHNOLOGY

Resistant Materials
Food Technology
Graphic Products
Textiles Technology
Product Design
Electronic Products

GEOGRAPHY

AQA Geography

CHILD DEVELOPMENT

Child Development

MODERN FOREIGN LANGUAGES

French
AQA French*
Spanish*
German*

BUSINESS STUDIES

Business Studies

PHYSICAL EDUCATION

Physical Education

SCIENCE

AQA Biology
AQA Chemistry
AQA Physics
AQA Science
AQA Additional Science
AQA Additional Applied Science
Edexcel Biology
Edexcel Chemistry
Edexcel Physics
Edexcel Science
Edexcel Additional Science
OCR A 21st Century Science
OCR A 21st Century Additional Science
OCR A 21st Century Additional Applied Science
OCR A 21st Century Biology
OCR A 21st Century Chemistry
OCR A 21st Century Physics
OCR B Gateway Biology
OCR B Gateway Chemistry
OCR B Gateway Physics
OCR B Gateway Science
OCR B Gateway Additional Science

*Workbooks not available for these titles

Buy online at www.lettsandlonsdale.com

Revise GCSE French

Revise GCSE has everything you need to achieve the grade you want. It will help to boost your learning and focus your revision.

- Exam board labels keep you on course
- Key points highlight the essential information
- Progress check questions test your learning
- Examples of controlled assessment tasks with model answers and examiner's hints to show how you can boost your grade
- GCSE-style questions provide crucial exam practice

Books in the series

Biology	ICT
Business Studies	Mathematics
Chemistry	AQA Mathematics
English and English Literature	Physical Education
AQA English and English Literature	Physics
French	Science
Geography	Additional Science
German	Spanish
History	

This guide is for the new GCSE French specifications and is suitable for students starting the course from September 2009 onwards. If you started the course before this date (e.g. in September 2008), you will be following a different specification and need the guide shown here instead:

Buy online at **www.lettsandlonsdale.com**   9781843155072

Visit **www.lettsandlonsdale.com**
for free education and revision advice

£14.99

ISBN 978-1-906415-
9 781906 415792 >